The 90th & 91st Aero Squadrons

The 90th & 91st Aero Squadrons

Two Accounts of American Pilots and Aircraft During the First World War

The Ninetieth Aero Squadron American Expeditionary Forces

Leland M. Carver, Gustaf A. Lindstrom and A. T. Foster

History of the 91st Aero Squadron Air Service U. S. A.

George C. Kenney and Horace Moss Guilbert

LEONAUR

The 90th & 91st Aero Squadrons
Two Accounts of American Pilots and Aircraft During the First World War
The Ninetieth Aero Squadron American Expeditionary Forces
by Leland M. Carver, Gustaf A. Lindstrom and A. T. Foster
History of the 91st Aero Squadron Air Service U. S. A.
by George C. Kenney and Horace Moss Guilbert

FIRST EDITION

First published under the titles
The Ninetieth Aero Squadron American Expeditionary Forces
and
History of the 91st Aero Squadron Air Service U. S. A.

Leonaur is an imprint
of Oakpast Ltd

ISBN: 978-1-78282-449-7 (hardcover)
ISBN: 978-1-78282-450-3 (softcover)

http://www.leonaur.com

Publisher's Notes

The views expressed in this book are not necessarily
those of the publisher.

Contents

The Ninetieth Aero Squadron American
Expeditionary Forces

Contents

To Our Loved Comrades
who gave their all, and
whose example and memory
inspired the rest of us to
carry on—
—this book is dedicated.

The History of the 90th Aero Squadron American Expeditionary Forces

The 90th Aero Squadron was created by Special Order 104, Headquarters Kelley Field, South San Antonio, Texas, on September 25, 1917. The men in it were largely from two detachments; one from Vancouver Barracks, Washington, which arrived at Kelley Field August 18; another from Fort Leavenworth, Kansas, which arrived August 25. Both of these detachments had been held from the date of their arrival until September 25 under Recruit Camp Headquarters as a Provisional Squadron. The day after the forming of the Squadron, September 26, 1917, under Special Order 119, Headquarters Kelley Field, Lieut. W. H.Y. Hackett took command. On September 28, Lieut. J.J. Livingston, M.R.C., with four enlisted men of the Medical Corps, were assigned to the 90th. Lieutenant Livingston has ever since been with the Squadron, save for the periods during which he was on detached service at hospitals.

This completed the primary organization of the enlisted part of the Squadron. Many changes were to take place in the course of the next year, but the foundation of the *esprit*, which was to be so great a factor in the Squadron's success on the front, was laid. Specialised training was necessary, but nearly all were by trade expert mechanics, who had volunteered for the work to which they had been assigned and who were enthusiastic over the prospect of doing their "bit" along the lines for which they were peculiarly fitted. It might be taken as an augury of success and as an indication of the adaptability of the 90th, that at this time every State of the Union was represented by one or more men.

On September 30, under command of Lieutenant Hackett, the Squadron left San Antonio for Mineola, Long Island, where it arrived five days later. Good order, good health and good spirits marked the whole trip. On the night of October 5 the Squadron detrained, and early next morning hiked out to Field No. 2 of the Aviation Mobilisation Camp, where they were quartered with the Headquarters of the First Provisional Wing in Barracks No. 5. Here they stayed for three weeks performing guard duty and fatigue work, and carrying on the work of organization, equipment and preparation for overseas duty. Recreation was provided in the form of frequent twenty-four hour passes to New York City and other towns in the neighbourhood, so that the time did not pass too slowly. It should be put on record that after the 90th had departed from Mineola its example was held up to succeeding squadrons as one worthy of emulation.

About the middle of October rumours began to circulate as to the early departure of the Squadron for overseas duty, but it was not till the 26th of the month that orders were received to pack up equipment and to prepare for immediate departure. The following day the Squadron entrained for Pier 54, North River, and boarded H.M.S. *Orduna*. Two officers and 157 men were at this time on the Squadron roster.

The crossing of the Atlantic was uneventful. The *Orduna* proceeded alone to Halifax, where It picked up seven other vessels and the convoy sailed together October 31 for Liverpool. Lieutenant Hackett was appointed Assistant Adjutant to Major Moynahan, 165th Infantry, who commanded the troops on board. The quarters furnished the men were fairly good, and only a few cases of "*mal de mer*" occurred during the two weeks on the boat. An occasional submarine alarm, which always proved to be false, helped to while away the time. Guard duty, and two daily inspections at 10 a.m. and 4 p.m. were the only other amusements.

On November 10 the *Orduna* moved into the dock at Liverpool, welcomed by numerous British ships in the harbour. Bands played, flags were run out, and the entry of the convoy seemed like a celebration. The troops were disembarked by three in the afternoon, and the 90th marched through the streets to the railroad station. It is safe to say that this first glimpse of a British city, and these first welcomes from a people as whose ally we had come to fight, made an impression which no man in the 90th will ever forget.

No stop was made in Liverpool; a train was waiting and the Squad-

FLYING FIELD AT OURCHES

ron was carried on to Southampton, and then given a march of an hour and a half to a "Rest Camp." Here the men first tried the British ration, and began to learn at first hand the hardships of the submarine blockade.

On November 12 the Squadron crossed the Channel on the transport *Prince George*, arriving in Havre early on the 13th, and marched at once to A.E.F. Rest Camp No. 2. Here they remained several days and the officers who had been temporarily attached at New York, as well as six first-class sergeants, were detached from the organization. On November 18 the 90th made the personal acquaintance of the famous *"Hommes 40, Chevaux"* box cars, entraining for Colombey les Belles, northeast of Neufchateau and south of Toul. After a long and tiresome trip, the destination was reached during the night of November 20, and the next morning the men were billeted In lofts scattered through the village.

It was now announced for the first time that the 90th was to do road and barracks construction work for the time being. Naturally this came as a great disappointment to all, as the great ambition of everyone had been to get into a service squadron, and do work on the front. However, the experience gained in construction work would be valuable, and the time could be profitably employed In fitting the right men into the right places. It was with these feelings that officers and men set to work on the first job assigned, the construction of roads through what was to become the great American Aviation Field at Colombey. This lasted the rest of the year. For the first three months of 1918 the Squadron, together with the 88th and 89th Squadrons, was to start the construction of the barracks and hangars of the Colombey Field. This was a piece of work of which the squadrons which took part might well be proud, as the buildings were erected with little delay in the very worst part of a particularly severe winter. The period of apprenticeship was now passed and the 90th was designated as a Service Squadron.

During this period of initiation to life in the A.E.F. there were many incidents which the men will be glad to remember in after years. On November 27, 1917, Lieutenant Schauffler, who was destined to command the Squadron during the greater part of its time at the front, brought by aeroplane the first mail it had received since leaving the States. That same night the British Aviation Field at Ochey, near by, was bombed, and the 90th saw from a distance a bit of the war. Thanksgiving Day was, of course, a holiday, and the 90th celebrated by beating the 2nd Engineers at football by a score of 12-0. On December 5, Colombey was treated to a German bombing raid, six bombs being dropped, one of them a dud. The only one which did much damage destroyed the house at No. 6 Rue Jeanne d'Arc and injured two Americans who were billeted there.

Christmas Day was observed in fitting manner. At 11 :30 a.m. the Squadron was formed at the Mess Hall and marched to Post Headquarters. Here the Stars and Stripes were unfurled. The Squadron then paraded through the village to the music of the 364th French Infantry, headed by Lieutenant Hackett. Then came a promotion ceremony by which four new sergeants, three corporals, and ten first-class privates were created. The Christmas dinner, with roast turkey as the principal dish, was a merry meal, and in the evening the Y. M. C. A. gave a musical entertainment in which 90th men took a large part.

On April 13 Major Dunsworth succeeded Lieutenant Hackett as commanding officer, as all Service Squadrons at the front must be commanded by flying officers. It is fitting here that a word of appreciation should be given Lieutenant Hackett for his work with the Squadron. He set the example of efficiency which the 90th has always followed. Through his efforts the personnel of the Squadron was picked and it was under his guidance that the Squadron started its career. His success in picking the Squadron was noteworthy, and the numerous trips by land and water which were made under his leadership went off most smoothly. At the same time, by his fairness and firmness, he made himself most popular with the men under his command. After Major Dunsworth took command Lieutenant Hackett remained with the Squadron as adjutant for four months. One thing which makes him unique among the rest of the 90th is the fact that he was the only one who was married while overseas. On October 1 he married an American girl who was at that time living in Paris. Unfortunately, Lieutenant Hackett had left the Squadron at that time and none of the officers were able to get to his wedding in Paris.

On April 15 the Squadron finally came into its own as a Service Squadron. Fifteen French Sopwith observation planes arrived from Paris and six pilots were assigned to the Squadron. These six, the first to fly for the 90th, were: Lieuts. "Judge" Hill, who was later shot down behind the German lines; "Ernie" Giroux, later shot down in flames; Cannon, Eaton, Jeffers, and Sherry. They had all received their entire training in the air in France. Jeffers, Cannon and Eaton were honour students of the first Ground School class graduated in the United

The "V" in the woods at Flirey

States; Hill and Giroux came to France in June, 1917, to join the La-fayette Escadrille, but enlisted instead in the American Air Service on arrival; "Madame" Sherry enlisted in Paris, having served previously as volunteer with the Transport Section of the American Field Service with the French armies.

No flying was done for the first few days after the arrival of the Sopwiths, but the mechanics were assigned to their respective planes and spent the time in studying their construction. On April 19 the Squadron moved to Amanty, north of Neufchateau, where the Ob-servation Training Centre of the 1st Corps was located. Here it was engaged in training flights. The flying personnel was changing con-stantly, pilots and observers being attached for a short time and then transferred to *chasse* or bombing squadrons. Naturally the breakage of planes was considerable, as most of the pilots had been trained on Nieuports, and the change to the Sopwiths proved difficult. No one, however, was seriously injured.

Meantime, the organisation of the Squadron as a fighting unit was continuing. On May 7 Lieutenant Looney joined as Supply Officer, a graduate of the Ground Officers' Training School at Kelley Field; Lieutenant O'Connor, Radio Officer, arrived May 13 from the Radio School at College Park, Maryland. Lieutenant Lacy reported on June 6 as Armament Officer after training at the Springfield Armoury.

On May 18 the following pilots reported for duty: Lieutenants Cowle, Conover, Ellis, Greist, Livingston, Neidecker, Patterson, Pier-son, Simpson, White, Freeman, Merz, Brewer, Lee, Pike, and Hathaway. Early in June the following observers reported: Lieutenants Adams, Francis, Maynor, Grainger, Bolt, Vinson, Blekre, Hendricks, Tillman, Shuss, Sherrick, Harrison, Lowe, Walden, and Sullivan, while Lieuten-ant Lockwood reported for duty as Engineering Officer, after hav-ing served for some time in that capacity at Field 7, Third Aviation Instruction Centre.

On June 13 the Squadron received its first assignment to active duty, moving to Ourches, fifteen kilometres due west of Toul, on the Meuse River, the station of the First Corps Observation Group. Like many divisions of Infantry the Squadron was to do its first real work in the famous "American" sector, which at that time extended from Apremont, east of St, Mihiel, to Remenauville, west of the Moselle. Here we were destined to remain for some time, till, from the air, every stick and stone of the sector became familiar to the pilots and observers, and the famous "V" in the woods north of Flirey was to

THE 90TH AT LIBOURNE, (GROUP 1)

direct many a pilot toward home and safety after his first trip over the lines.

The first mission to go over the lines was a general reconnaissance of the sector on June 16th by a formation consisting of Major Dunsworth, pilot, with Lieutenant Adams, observer, in No. 13, leading; Lieutenant White, pilot, with Lieutenant Hendricks, observer, in No. 7, and Lieutenant Simpson, pilot, with Captain Goss, observer, in No. 15. The reconnaissance covered the sector from Apremont to Xivray; the first compliments of the Hun to the 90th were received in the shape of an Archie barrage, which pierced Lieutenant White's plane in several places. Anti-aircraft fire over Apremont was reported to be particularly accurate by all, a note which became a stock feature of observers' reports in the succeeding months.

Later In the day another formation went out, led by Lieutenant Greist, in plane No. 4, with Lieutenant Vinson as observer; Lieutenant Neidecker, pilot, with Lieutenant Tillman, observer, in No. 5; Lieutenants Patterson and Blekre, in No. 14; Lieutenants Ellis and Shuss, in No. 17, and Lieutenants Pierson and Maynor, in No. 6. The following day six missions were carried out over the sector, but for the rest of the month little work was done, as the sector was quiet and there were three squadrons to divide the work.

On June 20 Lieut. W. G. Schauffler took command, *vice* Major Dunsworth, who left to take a course in aerial gunnery at Caseaux. This appointment was made permanent when Major Dunsworth was assigned in his absence to the command of the 96th Aero Squadron. Lieutenant Schauffler came to the 90th from the First Observation Squadron. With this squadron he had seen service on the Mexican border and had the honour of being the first pilot of an American squadron to fly over the front. Other important additions to the Squadron during this period were made by the arrival of Lieutenant Young on June 19, Lieutenant Rohrer on June 26, and Lieutenants Bovard and Kinsley on July 3.

On June 25 the first casualties occurred in the Squadron, caused by an accident. Lieutenants Hathaway, pilot, and Maynor, observer, started at 8 a.m. on a reconnaissance mission. Hardly had they left the field when, from an altitude of 200 metres, their plane went into a *vrille* and dove into the ground with full motor. Both were killed instantly. The funeral was held at Sebastopol, near Toul, and was attended by all. Lieutenants Pierson and Harrison circled overhead in a plane and at the close of the service dropped flowers on the grave.

The death of these two men, coming so soon after the arrival of the Squadron on the front, was very keenly felt. Both had been among the first in France, and left a host of friends who will long remember them.

Lieutenant Hathaway came to France early in 1917 as a volunteer in the American Field Service. His whole training in aviation was in France, beginning with the French Caudron School at Tours, in the early part of September. From this he graduated in the latter part of October and went to the American School for Advanced Training at Issoudun. He left there in January, 1918, to go to the American Observers School at Tours, there assisting in the instruction of observers, going from there directly to the front in May, where he joined the 90th at Amanty.

Lieutenant Maynor arrived in France in September, 1917, and after some weeks at an Artillery School, was assigned to the 101st Field Artillery. He was a member of the first class in the school for aerial observers at Tours, which began work on January 14, 1918. After graduating, on February 22, he proceeded to the First Corps Observation Training Centre at Amanty. From there he was ordered to a French Observation Squadron with the Eighth Army. After several weeks there, he took the course in aerial gunnery at Cazeaux, and on its completion reported for duty with the 90th.

The Fourth of July was fittingly celebrated in several ways; a flag raising was held; Secretary Walker of the Y. M. C. A. read the Declaration of Independence, and Lieutenant Mahan, Post Adjutant, delivered an address. Lieutenant Schauffler then went out in a biplane Spad to celebrate in the air, accompanied by Lieutenant Harrison. They recalled the meaning of the day to the Germans by strafing several towns, and on the way home joined in the celebrations which were being held by the French in Toul, Commercy and Void, flying just over the tree tops and waving to the people in the streets below.

Other additions were made to the flying personnel during this period. Lieutenant Bogle joined the Squadron on July 4. On July 13 Lieutenants Parr, Lindstrom, Borden, and Hayden, observers, arrived. Lieutenant Carver, pilot, reported July 19, and Lieutenant Derby, observer, on the 23rd. On the 24th Lieutenant Schauffler was suddenly taken ill and had to be removed to the hospital. He was temporarily replaced in command by Lieutenant Gallup, also of the 1st Aero Squadron, who retained command till September 15. Lieutenant Wallace joined the Squadron on August 24, replacing Lieutenant Lockwood as

The 90th at Libourne, (Group 2)

Engineering Officer, he becoming temporarily Transportation Officer. Lieutenant Wallace had trained in the Aviation Engineering School at the Massachusetts Institute of Technology, and very soon after his arrival with the 90th made a record for upkeep of motors and planes which no other Squadron has ever surpassed. On the departure of Lieutenant Hackett, Lieutenant Lockwood was made Adjutant.

The work during July was the regular aerial work for a Corps Squadron on a quiet sector. Two regular reconnaissances were made each day and during good weather photographic missions were carried out. The 90th was alone on the field and took care of all the work assigned to the 4th Corps Observation Group.

The French Sopwiths, with which the Squadron did all their early work, never proved very satisfactory on the front. They were rather slow, and their elastic construction never inspired a great deal of confidence. Hence it was with great relief that the Squadron saw the "Sops" being replaced with other ships, though at first these latter were of several types, and made of the 90th the strangest hybrid Squadron in the A.E.F. Early in July a few biplane Spads arrived. On July 19 the first of the Salmsons arrived, piloted from Colombey by Lieutenant Cowle, and it was rapidly followed by others. Shortly afterward three Breguets were assigned to us, so that on July 31 the Squadron equipment included sixteen Salmsons, eight Sopwiths, four Spads, and three Breguets. This was an assortment which must have given many a German Intelligence Officer some hard moments identifying.

The object of the Breguets was to give the Squadron practice in night flying. This had been attempted in Sopwiths, but had resulted only in the salvaging of numerous machines. After the arrival of the Breguets the experiment was once more undertaken, but without success. The field was absolutely unsuited for any such work. It was on top of a hill which sloped precipitously on all sides into deep valleys. Consequently, in landing in the dark, there was a great tendency to underestimate the slope, and a crash into the side of the hill was the natural consequence. Fortunately, no one was seriously hurt in this work; the worst injuries were received by Major Anderson, who received a cut on the face when he, with Lieutenant Kirwan, Group Observation Officer, as observer, crashed into the hill in landing. The only really successful night flight was made by Lieutenants Young and Harrison, who went up with the idea of protecting the field against bombing raids, and after staying up for over an hour, made a good landing. After two of the Breguets had been salvaged, the remaining one was rescued by an order suspending the experiment.

On the night of July 31, at about half past ten, the 90th was host to a small German bombing party. The officers and men heard the planes overhead, and identified them as German by the sound of their motors, which were suddenly cut, and the machines glided down toward the field, heading toward the Spad hangar. They dropped seven small bombs, three of which landed within twenty feet of the hangars; but by great good fortune did no damage beyond a few holes In the field, and these were filled in before daylight in order that no photographic reconnaissance by the Germans would reveal how close they came to accomplishing their end.

It was about this time that the division of the squadron into flights was made. Lieutenants White, Greist, and Pierson were appointed commanders of A, B, and C Flights, respectively. At the same time the flights selected their colours: A Flight, white, probably in compliment to its commander; B Flight, orange, and C Flight, red.

On August 4 the first Infantry Contact mission was assigned to the 90th, the work of which it was later to do so much, and by which it gained its reputation of being a "Shock Squadron." A "*coup de main*" by the infantry was being carried out northeast of Flirey. Lieutenants White and Sherrick were detailed to carry out the mission at dawn and report on the attainment of the objective four kilometres beyond the old German lines. In spite of extremely bad weather conditions, a contrary wind and low clouds with frequent showers, the mission was quite successful, and valuable information as to the progress of the raid was brought back.

In the early part of August the 135th Aero Squadron joined the 90th at Ourches, and for the balance of the month the Corps work was split between the two Squadrons. The 135th was the first Squadron on the front with the American-built De Haviland 4's with Liberty motors, and as such created considerable attention. Their first flight over the lines was on August 10. As they were new to the sector, they requested Lieutenant White of the 90th to take the place of one of their pilots who was ill, and to lead their formation. This he did. Weather conditions were unfavourable, and the formation broke up, but to Lieutenant White belongs the distinction of having taken the first Liberty over the active front.

In addition to the regular corps work which the 90th was doing, they carried out a considerable number of Infantry Contact patrols near Chaumont, taking part in exercises with newly arrived divisions.

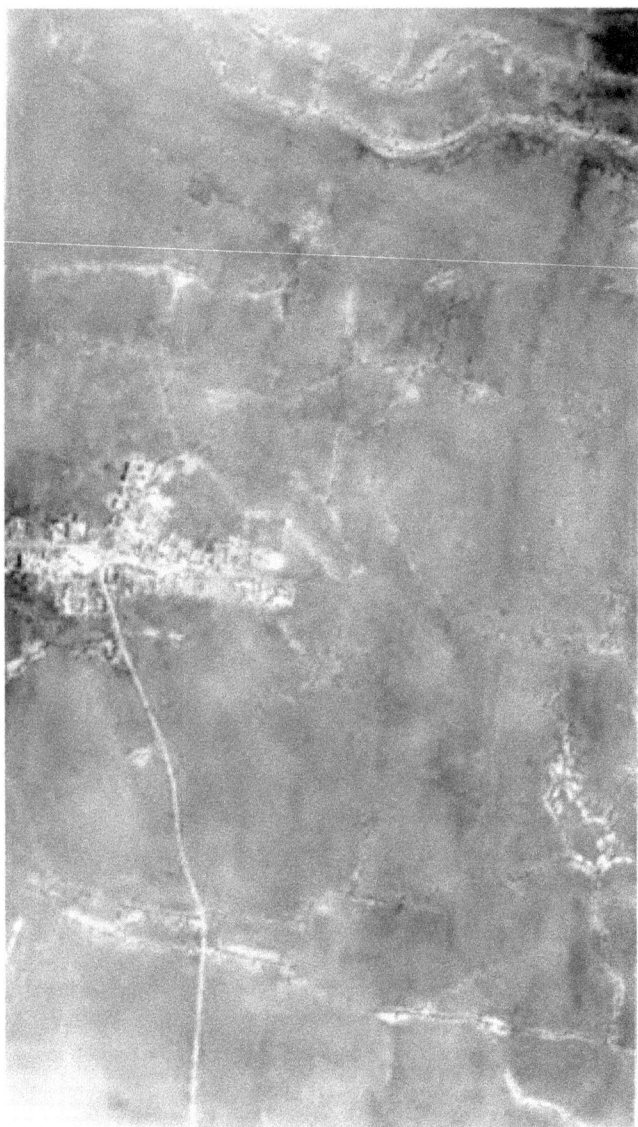

XIVRAY (ST. MIHIEL SECTOR)

A few adjustments of artillery with French batteries in the woods north of Boucq were also carried out.

On September 7 Lieutenants Lake, Burger, and Grier joined the Squadron. They had served several months with the French Caudron 46 Escadrille as Machine Gunners and had flown on many protection flights for daylight bombing raids. They had all been decorated with the *Croix de Guerre*. Lieutenants Hart, Broomfield, and Dorrance arrived from pilots' school on the same day.

The first work of great importance which came to the Squadron was its part in the operations which resulted in the clearing of the St. Mihiel salient, September 12-14, 1918. The two weeks preceding were spent in much careful preparatory work. A great deal of photographic work was done, among other missions being the photographing of the lines from Apremont to Limy at an altitude of 350 metres, by Lieutenant Lindstrom, observer, and Lieutenant Carver, pilot. Maps were prepared with great care and all was made ready for "D" day and "H" hour. On September 12 the 90th had available for duty eighteen pilots, thirteen observers, and three machine gunners. The Squadron had twenty-five Salmsons on hand, all of which were available for duty. The planes were all armed with Vickers guns firing through the propeller for the pilot, and two Lewis flexible guns for the observer, these being mounted on a tourelle.

Two days before the attack each team was assigned to its particular duty during the attack. Every man became absorbed in studying his particular task. From then on, till "H" hour arrived, the enthusiasm and earnest endeavour of every man in the Squadron seemed to charge the atmosphere with a spirit that spelled success. The under current of enthusiasm revealed itself particularly at the Squadron mess. The spirit of the 90th and its determination to "do" was evidenced in the songs, the toasts, and the general feeling of good-fellowship which pervaded the atmosphere at mess. With such a spirit success was bound to come.

The night of September 11 was one which will always remain fixed in the memory of the flying officers; pilots and observers were called together about 8 p.m., as soon as it was definitely learned that the attack would be made the next day. Major McNarney, the group commander, gave the group a few last hints as to the methods to be used in their work. Aviation, he said, was a very essential part of the attack, and whatever the weather, the missions were to be performed as long as it was physically possible for the planes to take off.

VERDUN

It was known that the barrage was to be a particularly dense one, but there must be no hesitation to go through it. From conversation with French officers the impression had been gained that infantry contact was at best a hazardous game; that any team that carried out more than one was entitled to the greatest credit, and could have done it only because favoured by chance. As three trips were scheduled for each man on the following day, there seemed to be need of great good luck for the Squadron to come through unscathed.

The day finally arrived and with it probably the worst weather in which a Squadron ever attempted to carry on major aerial operations. The first mission, an infantry liaison—Lieutenant Rohrer, pilot, with Lieutenant Vinson as observer—left the ground at 5:20 a.m., in spite of a high west wind and a ceiling of about 300 metres. These conditions prevailed throughout the greater part of the day, with low-hanging, heavy clouds and intermittent, heavy showers. The 90th was working with the famous 42nd or Rainbow Division, and throughout the course of the day's advance faithfully recorded the progress made by the Infantry, and was practically the only reliable liaison between the advancing troops and the Division Headquarters.

As was to be expected, flying at such extremely low altitudes, due to the clouds and rain, the 90th planes were not to get through the day untouched. Early in the day, Lieutenant Young, pilot, and Lieutenant Bogle, observer, had the radiator of their plane pierced by machine gun bullets fired from the ground, while flying at an altitude of about 50 metres in the vicinity of Thiaucourt. So near were they to crashing behind the German lines that at one time, with the wheels of the plane nearly on the ground, the German infantrymen ran In their direction, expecting the plane to crash In a shell hole. However, Lieutenant Young brought the plane back into friendly territory, finally landing just behind the advancing American lines. They at once delivered their information, and then, making use of any transportation going toward the Squadron, they made their way back in time for Lieutenant Bogle to go up on another mission late in the afternoon.

Lieutenant Kinsley, with Lieutenant Lowe, observer, had a similar experience while carrying out an infantry contract mission later In the day, but being nearer to our lines when it happened. Lieutenant Kinsley was able to bring the plane back as far as Corps Headquarters, where they landed and delivered their information.

On September 12 the 90th made twenty-six sorties, and in no case did a plane fail to carry out its mission successfully.

September 13, the second day of the attack, was very much a repetition of the first day. The infantry continued to advance, attaining their forty-eight-hour objective in twenty-seven hours, and the Squadron planes reported the progress of the troops from hour to hour.

In the attack the chief work of the observers consisted of finding and reporting to the rear the position of our front line, the location of hostile strong points, surveillance for enemy counter-attack, and the harassing of the retreating enemy by machine gun fire.

September 15 Lieutenant Schauffler returned from the hospital and assumed command.

The following letters of appreciation were received by the Squadron as a result of the satisfactory work done by the Squadron during the attack:

Headquarters 67th F. A. Brigade
American Expeditionary Forces
France

September 15, 1918.

From: The Adjutant.
To: Commanding Officer, 90th Aero Squadron, 4th Obs. Group.
Subject: Recent Operations.
1. The Brigade Commander directs me to express to you his appreciation of the efficient service of your Squadron in connection with this brigade during the recent operations in the St. Mihiel salient. The service of your command has been most efficient and satisfactory.

C. H. Nance,
Major, F. A., U. S. A.

American Expeditionary Forces

September 15, 1918.

From: Commanding General, 42nd Division
To: Chief of Air Service, Amer. E. F.
Subject: . Expression of Appreciation.
1. It is desired to express appreciation of the work done by the 90th Aero Squadron, 4th Corps, Observation Group, during the recent operations. This Squadron, continually on duty, rendered most excellent service to the division in furnishing valuable information promptly with regard to the advance made by our own elements and movements of enemy forces; also in regulat-

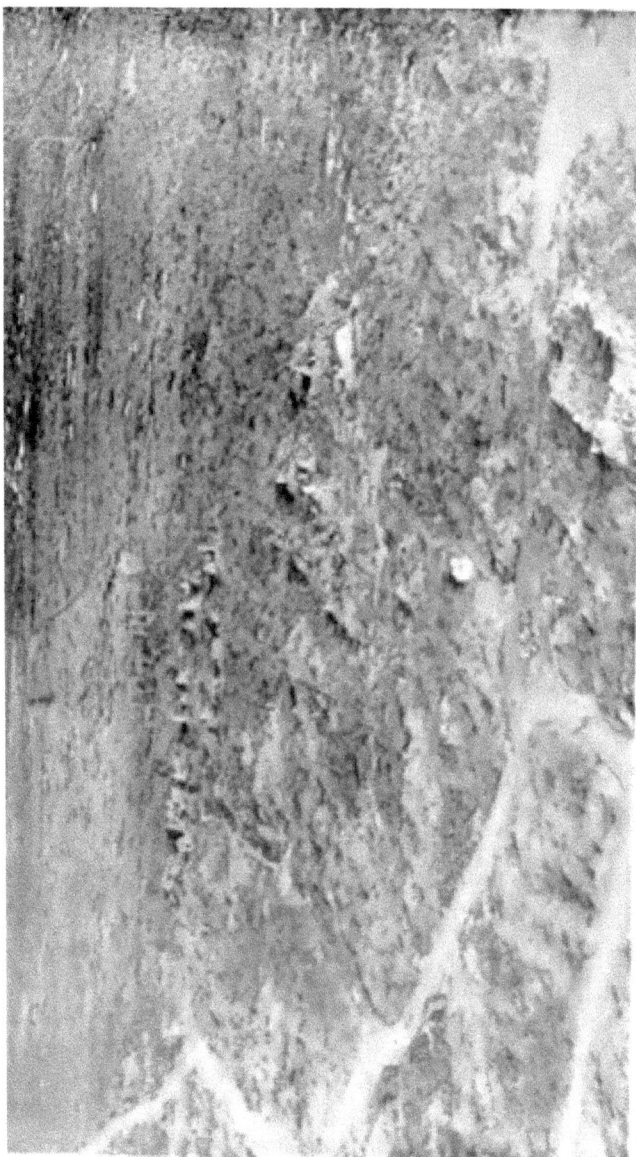

BETHINCOURT (ARGONNE-MEUSE SECTOR)

ing our artillery fire and the spotting of fugitive targets.

(Signed)   Chas. T. Menoher,
                            Major General, U. S. A.

American Expeditionary Forces
Office of Chief of Air Service
                            September 25, 1918.

From: C A. S.
To: Commanding Officer, 90th Aero Squadron
        (Through C. A. S., 4th Corps).
Subject: Appreciation.
1. I take great pleasure in transmitting to you a letter of appreciation from the Commanding General, 42nd Division, for the excellent work done by your Squadron during the recent operations.
2. This appreciation may have already reached you, but the Chief of the Air Service takes great pleasure in adding his appreciation to that of the Commanding General, 42nd Division, and in thanking you and the officers and men under your command for the fine part you and they have played in the recent operations. By direction of the C. A. S.,

                            H. C. Whitehead,
                            Colonel, A. S

Headquarters Air Service
4th Army Corps
                            October 1, 1918.

From: Chief of Air Service, 4th Army Corps.
To: Commanding Officer, 90th Aero Squadron
        (Through C. O. Observation Group, 3rd Army Corps).
Subject: Appreciation.
1. I wish to forward the enclosed letter of appreciation with my congratulations. It is a great pleasure to command units which conduct themselves as the 90th did during the St. Mihiel operations.

(Signed)   H. B. Anderson,
                            Major, Air Service, U. S. A.

From September 15 to 20 the Squadron made several daily reconnaissances of its sector and carried out several photographic missions. On September 13 Lieutenant Carver, Pilot, and Lieutenant Lindstrom, Observer, took oblique views of the various towns in the 42nd

FLYING FIELD AT SOUILLY

Division's sector of the salient, and on September 15 photographed the Hindenburg Line from Rembercourt to the Lac de La Chaussee, both missions being carried out from an altitude of 300 metres. On September 16 Lieutenant Pierson, Pilot, and Lieutenant Hayden, Observer, although harassed by intense Archie fire, photographed the Hindenburg Line and territory in the rear of the German lines. On September 14 Lieutenant Conover, Pilot, and Lieutenant Lindstrom, Observer, started on a photo mission which covered the territory in the rear of the lines between Rembercourt and La Chaussee. They started out with chasse protection, but for some reason these planes soon became separated from them; nevertheless, they continued the mission and completed it successfully.

On September 20 the Squadron moved from Ourches to Souilly, southwest of Verdun, transferring from the 4th Corps to the 3rd Corps, First Army. With this it was to work during the Argonne-Meuse offensive, which terminated only with the armistice. In spite of the long distance which the Squadron moved, there was no great delay in activity, and in a day or so the Squadron was operating on the new sector. From September 22 to 26 the Squadron made only short reconnaissance flights back of the American lines to acquaint the flying personnel with the new sector. This was in order that the enemy might not notice increased aerial activity on the sector and foresee the coming attack.

On September 24 Captain Foster, and Lieutenants Cutter, Foster, and Elliott, joined the Squadron. As there were then no vacancies In the teams, they were left temporarily without definite assignments.

The American First Army struck the first blow of the Argonne-Meuse offensive on the morning of September 26, and offensive operations continued almost without cessation until November 11. At the start the 90th was operating with two divisions of the 3rd Corps, but on October 11, one-half of the Squadron was assigned to duty with the 17th French Corps on the east bank of the Meuse. The Squadron continued to operate from the airdrome at Souilly, under orders of the Third Observation Group, Captain Littauer commanding.

The Squadron worked with the 80th Division from September 26 to October 11; with the 33rd from September 26 to October 22; on the west bank of the Meuse. On October 11 the 5th Division relieved the 80th and we continued our work with It. On October 22 the Squadron was attached to the 90th Division, on the west bank of the Meuse, and In the neighbourhood of Romagne and eastward. In place

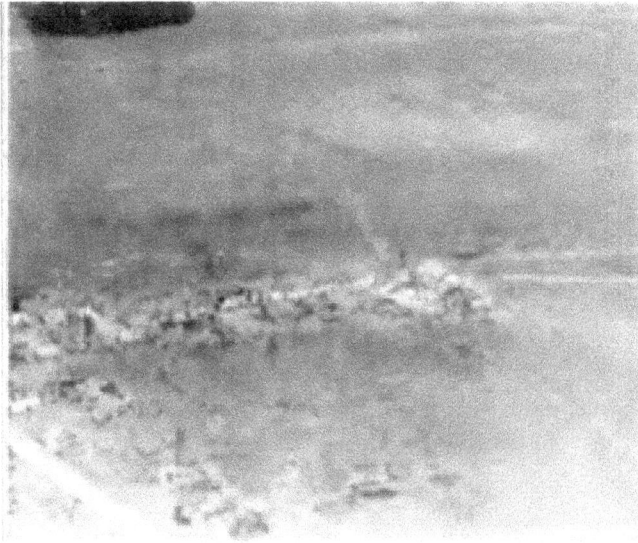

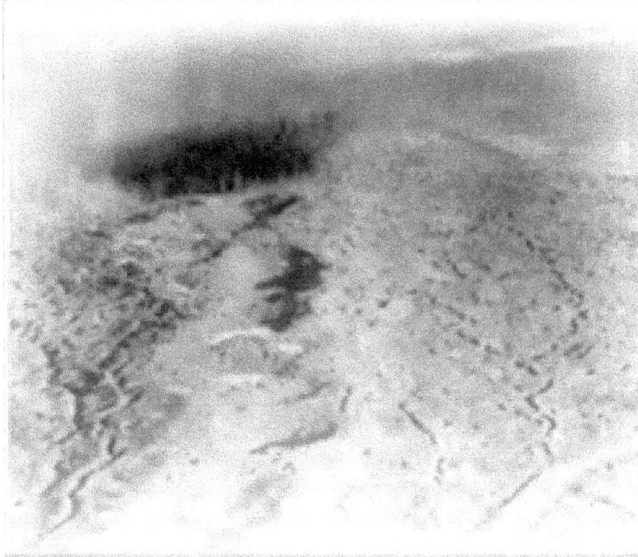

CUNEL (ARGONNE-MEUSE SECTOR)
MINE CRATERS (ARGONNE FOREST)

of the 5th Division. Till October 22 the Squadron worked with the 29th Division on the east bank of the Meuse, until this division was relieved by the 79th, with whom work was continued until the cessation of hostilities. The Squadron also continued work with the 90th Division until November 11.

During this time the closest possible relations were maintained between the Squadron and the divisions with which it was working, by the Squadron's liaison officers maintained at Divisional Headquarters. This was an experiment never tried before September 12, and was to improve the understanding between the Aviation and the Line. It had been found that line officers did not understand the nature of aerial work, and that communication between divisions and their supporting Squadrons was often too slow. Lieutenant Frances and Lieutenant Vinson eventually became our liaison officers. They remained constantly at the headquarters of the divisions with which we were working, reporting daily to the Squadron Operations officer by telephone, and rendered invaluable aid in maintaining close relations between the units.

The 3rd Corps Group at the same time established a Liaison School for the officers of the divisions with which it was working. Detachments from the 5th, 33rd, and 90th Divisions, each of about two hundred men and several officers, spent in turn several days with the group, the officers being entertained by the 90th Squadron during their stay. The training was doubtless of value and the intimacy which grew up between the men on the ground and the men In the air certainly increased the Interest each took in the work of the other.

As in the St. Mihiel operations, the Squadron had to contend with very bad weather. Owing to the season of the year and the proximity of the Meuse River Valley, the atmospheric conditions were almost always unfavourable. Heavy clouds and constant rains increased the difficulty of reconnaissances. The ground mists of the mornings, which seldom cleared up before 10 or 11 o'clock, added much to the difficulty. But in spite of the poor visibility which made the average altitude at which the planes could work about 300 metres, several daily reconnaissances were made.

Flying at a very low altitude, the Squadron planes daily penetrated the hostile lines to a depth of from three to five kilometres, bringing back information as to our own front line, position of hostile troops, batteries in action, fires, explosions, etc., and frequently a collection of bullet holes in the plane. This is considered probably the most dangerous and difficult work an Observation Squadron has to perform.

Artillery work was not as successful as infantry. This was chiefly due to bad weather, which made it impossible to attain the necessary altitude. When a clear day would finally come, the batteries would perhaps be moving or be found unable for some reason or another to carry out the *reglage* desired.

October 17, Lieutenant Adams, who had been Operations officer since June, left to become instructor in the aerial gunnery school at St. Jean du Mont. When Lieutenant Adams came to the Squadron he had had very little experience on the front, and the position of Operations officer is one which, more than any other, requires an intimate knowledge of observation work. In spite of this, he handled the mass of detail constantly passing through his hands with accuracy and dispatch, and never was any fault found with the way in which the 90th did its work under his superintendence. It was said of "Mort" that he would ask no one to undertake a mission which he would not undertake himself. And when a particularly dangerous or difficult mission was in hand, it was usually "Mort" who went out.

On October 22 Lieutenant Schauffler received his captaincy, and was at about the same time made group commander. The Squadron was sorry to lose the C.O., with whom they had worked so long and harmoniously over the front, but glad to see his merit recognised by the promotion. As a pilot, Captain Schauffler was second to none in skill and experience, and he loved the game. While in the hospital in September, he heard of the drive being made at St. Mihiel, and though only convalescent at the time, he ran away from the hospital, and arrived back at the Squadron in time to take an active part in the drive. "Schauff" was always most popular with the officers and men, and besides looking after the numerous details incidental to the running of the Squadron efficiently, he took an active part in the performance of missions over the lines.

Numerous other changes took place. Lieut. Norris E. Pierson, who had been with the Squadron since the Amanty days, and who was thoroughly familiar with the personnel, system and traditions of the Squadron, assumed command. Captain Schauffler took with him Lieutenant "Charlie" Lockwood, who had served the Squadron both as engineering officer, transportation officer, and adjutant, and had made an enviable record for zeal and efficiency in each capacity. He became group adjutant. Lieutenants Tillman and Sherrick also went with the group as operations officer and assistant operations officer,

90TH OFFICERS, NOV 11, 11 A.M.—THE HOUR OF THE ARMISTICE

respectively. Lieutenant Walden left the Squadron to become operations officer of the 93rd Aero Squadron. Lieut. "Marine" Lowe became squadron operations officer, and Lieutenant Hayden became adjutant. Lieutenant Whitehead joined the Squadron as pilot.

October 21 marked a very sad event in the history of the Squadron—the death of Lieutenants Broomfield and Cutter over the lines. They left the field at about 10 a.m. on an infantry contact mission, to discover whether our troops had taken Hill 299, east of the Bois de Rappes. They never returned, and it is believed were shot down by machine gun fire from the ground. In November, when our troops advanced, the wrecked plane was found on Hill 299, and Lieutenants Cutter and Broomfield were given a proper burial at Souilly.

Lieutenant Broomfield had graduated from Tours and Issoudun as observation pilot, and had taken the aerial gunnery course at Cazeaux. While he had been with the Squadron, he had frequently demonstrated his skill as a pilot and his efficiency was proved by his able management of the field at Ourches during the St. Mihiel drive.

Lieutenant Cutter was in the Minnesota National Guards at the outbreak of the war, and served as an officer in the Artillery until detailed in January to take the Aerial Observer's course at Fort Sill, Oklahoma. After graduating there he attended the Gunnery School at Fort Worth, Texas; then, coming to France in July, he took a short course at Tours in observation and gunnery, and proceeded directly to the Squadron at Souilly.

On October 28, Lieutenants Conover and Burger were out on an infantry contact mission, and were diving on enemy machine gun nests which were holding up the advance of the infantry, when machine gun bullets from the ground severely wounded Lieutenant Conover in the knee. In spite of this, he flew the plane back to our lines and managed to land safely without crashing, on the west bank of the Meuse, about five kilometres behind our front lines. They brought back valuable information which was at once transmitted to Division Headquarters, after which Lieutenant Conover was taken to the hospital, and has since been unable to rejoin the Squadron, being invalided back to the States. He had always been the one to start the song after the dinner table had been cleared, and his absence was felt as a keen loss by all.

As a result of the good work done by the Squadron during the October operations north of Verdun, it received the following letters of commendation from the 33rd Division, with which it had worked:

Headquarters 33rd Division
American Expeditionary Forces
France

October 20, 1918.

From: Commanding General, 33rd Division.
To: Commanding Officer, 90th Aero Squadron,
     Amer. E. F.
Subject: Service with 33rd Division.
1. As the 33rd Division is about to withdraw from this section of the line, I imagine the services with the division of the 90th Aero Squadron will end, at least for the time being. Consequently I wish to express to you at this time my appreciation for the valuable and efficient work the Squadron has done with us during the operations. You have met all our requests with willing compliance unless prevented unquestionably by the elements. Your greatest cooperation has been in assisting us in locating our lines, which you have done repeatedly with uniform success and accuracy.

George Bell, Jr.,
Major General, U. S. A.

West Bank of River,
30th Sept., 1918.

90th Aero Squadron.
Gentlemen: Many thanks for cigarettes and newspapers dropped to us. It sure made us feel fine to know that others were thinking of us. These are the things that make us want to go ahead. Sincerely,

Louis Preston,
Capt. 131st Inf.
Commanding Co. B, 33rd Division.

G-1   October 15, 1918.
General Orders No. 135
Officers, non-commissioned officers and enlisted men of the 29th and 33rd.
D.LU.S., 18th, 26th, D.L and 10th, D.I.C.
You have conquered Lawavrille, the wood Des Caures and that of D'Haumont, you have reached the summit of Ormont, gone beyond the Rechene and the woods of Chaume.
The Austro-Germans have lost, on curved front of 15 kilome-

tres, those arrogant observation posts which have defied the heroic defenders of Verdun.

On the 8th of October you advanced in a magnificent manner, on formidable slopes and through powerful and echelon organisations.

On the following day you pursued an obstinate advance which checked all the enemy counter-attacks; you compelled him to bring up numerous reinforcements in a hurry, which did not succeed in taking back one foot of conquered ground.

5,800 prisoners, more than 50 guns, machine guns and material which has not yet been counted, are the booty of these magnificent days.

All of you infantrymen, artillerymen, engineers, aviators, staff and other branches of the service have their part in the success.

American soldiers, French white and black soldiers, you have vied with each other in valour and comradeship during the combat, and weakened the menace which still threatens the Immortal City.

I am proud to have you under my command.

Commanding General of 17th French Corps.

(Signed)   Claudel.

Translated from the French by order of Captain Vignon,

C.A.S., 17th French Corps.   J. Tongas,

First Lieut. F.A., French Liaison Officer.

Owing to the rapid advance which the American First Army had made up to the last of October and the still more rapid advance which was contemplated, it was decided to be necessary for the 3rd Corps Group to be nearer the front line. Near Bethelainville was a high plateau which had previously been known as the only place in the sector where a forced landing could be made with any safety. It was far from level, very muddy, and had many shell holes. After the first drive, however, it was out of range of all but the heaviest artillery, so it was this field which was chosen. Barracks and hangars were erected in the Bois de Hesse, a stone road built leading up to the field, and on October 29 the 90th moved up. The 88th, 284th (French), and Group Headquarters followed a few days later.

The 90th was complimented by Corps Headquarters for the manner in which work was continued without interruption during the moving. Several planes took off in the morning from the Souilly field, and after accomplishing their missions, landed on the new field and made their reports.

Operations from Bethelainville proved most difficult. The field was isolated from all bases of supplies, the very uneven terrain was the cause of constant breakage of axles, and the mud made the transportation of supplies impossible without the use of caterpillar tractors.

While here, the last remaining team of those formed in August was broken up. Lieutenants Carver and Lindstrom set out on a reconnaissance the morning of November 4. The cloud level was at 200 metres, and just after diving through these clouds at a point a few miles north of Cunel, the front cowl suddenly blew off, and back into the flying wires, probably through the wire holding it having been cut. Lieutenant Carver attempted to land, after pointing the plane south, but either because of the added wind resistance from the hanking cowl, or through the elevator wires having been cut by fire from the ground, it was impossible to redress for the landing, and the plane crashed nose first into a shell hole north of Cunel. Lieutenant Carver's injuries were quite serious, among them a dislocated hip, sprained knee and ankle, and severe cuts on the face. Lieutenant Lindstrom's face was cut and bruised, but otherwise he was all right. The plane was totally demolished, the fuselage breaking in two pieces near the pilot's seat. Lieutenant Carver was discharged from the hospital January 7, 1919, and rejoined the Squadron at Belrain, Meuse.

The 90th reported constantly on the progress of the 90th and 79th Divisions during the stirring days just before the armistice, and rendered valuable aid in harassing the retreating Boche troops in their flight northward. Lieutenant Greist, with Lieutenant Wilkinson, Observer, in a flight made a day or so before the armistice, gave material assistance to a platoon of the 314th Infantry (79th Division), which had gotten into difficulty, and later discovered that it was commanded by Lieutenant Pierson, brother of our commanding officer.

Following the armistice little flying was done, most of the old pilots and observers being absent on leave or returning to the States. Lieutenant Greist, with Lieutenant Stevens, photographic officer of the 3rd Corps Observation Group, took some very fine oblique views of the devastated country north of Verdun, as well as of Verdun itself, while the pilots who arrived at the Squadron at the time of the armistice or later, amused themselves by wrecking most of the remaining planes and some of the new observers. The Squadron received word that it was to return to the States, surely a thing not to be regarded lightly, and the rest of the planes were turned in to the 1st Air Depot, and by January 15 practically all of the pilots and observers had been detached from the Squadron, which at that time found itself at Belrain, near Bar-le-Duc, whence it had moved from Bethelainville.

January 18 the Squadron took another step toward home, moving to Colombey les Belles, where it had commenced the building, in November, 1917, of the 1st Air Depot. Very comfortable quarters were assigned and the Squadron settled down to await orders to the coast.

The following are the officers who accompanied the Squadron to Libourne:

First Lieut. Norris E. Pierson, A.S. U.S.A., Commanding Officer.

First Lieut. E. Harold Greist, A.S. U.S.A., Adjutant and Flight Commander.

First Lieut. Loren E. Rohrer, A.S. U.SA., Flight Commander.
First Lieut. Leland M. Carver, A.S. U.S.A., Flight Commander.

First Lieut. William O. Lowe, U.S.M.C, Operations Officer.

First Lieut. Glenn M. Pike, A.S. U.S.A., Pilot.

First Lieut. J. J. Livingston, M.C. U.S.A., Surgeon.

First Lieut. Ralph G. Looney, A.S. U.S.A., Supply Officer.

Second Lieut. John H. Wallace, A.S. U.S.A., Engineering Officer.

Second Lieut. Clive W. Lacy, Ord. U.S.A., Ordnance Officer.

Second Lieut. Arthur J. O'Connor, A.S. U.S.A., Radio Officer.

The Squadron left Colombey les Belles January 25, 1919, *en route* for the port of embarkation. The travel directed was accomplished in the French variety of Side-door Pullmans, otherwise known to fame as "*Hommes 40, Chevaux 8*," and was said to be necessary in the military service. Through the initiative of our men stoves were installed, which made the journey bearable in spite of the considerable cold weather encountered. Our actual destination proved to be the pretty little village of St. Denis de Piles, near Libourne, Gironde, and the officers and enlisted personnel occupied excellent billets, which had been arranged for by the advance party under command of Lieutenant Rohrer.

On February 3, after five days spent at St. Denis, the Squadron was

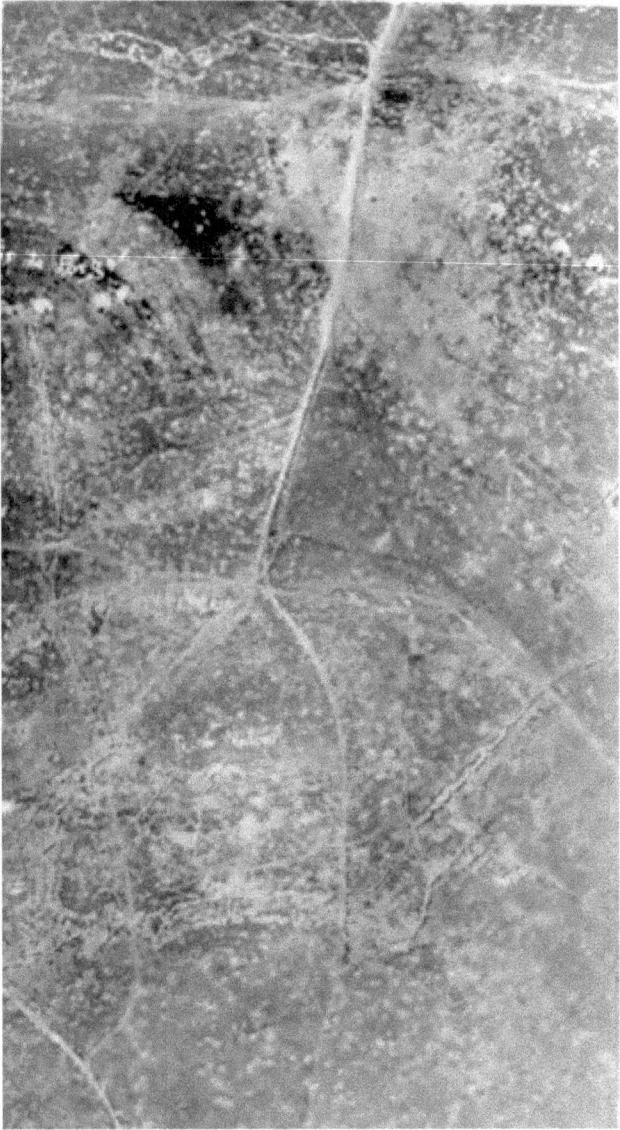

Bois de Forges (Meuse Sector)

ordered to Libourne, the next step on the way home. There we occupied the old stone French barracks, while the officers were billeted at private houses throughout the town. The time was spent in drilling, fatigue work, and other recreation, including the famous outdoor sport of "making big ones into little ones," which the men all thoroughly enjoyed. (???).

On February 22, Lieutenant Pierson received his promotion to a captaincy, for which he and the flight commanders had been recommended prior to the armistice.

March 10, Lieutenant Pike left the Squadron to proceed to Poland as a member of the American Food Commission, and shortly after Lieut. J. J. Livingston, our medical officer since the formation of the Squadron at Kelley Field, left to take a course of study at the A.E.F. University at Beaume. March 21, Lieutenant Greist, who had been a flight commander since the Squadron arrived at the front, and who had served as adjutant since shortly after the armistice, was detached to go home as a casual, on account of the receipt of news of illness in his family. Lieutenant Rohrer was appointed Adjutant to succeed him.

On April 10, Lieutenant Lowe learned from a Navy Department order that he had been a captain since July 8, 1918.

The Squadron remained at Libourne until April 10, when the long-awaited order to proceed to the Embarkation Camp at last arrived. The trip to Genicart was made in one day by marching, and the Squadron entered Camp No. 1, the first stage in the process through the Embarkation Camp. After two days here, the next step was taken, the Squadron going to Camp No. 2, entering by way of the "mill," where delousing and the physical examinations took place. All the members of the 90th were pronounced "fit," and there remained only to wait for the boat to be designated.

After two or three disappointments we were ordered on board the U.S.S. *General Goethals,* but unfortunately, owing to the small size of the boat and the consequent limitations in staterooms for the officers, the Squadron was allowed to take but three officers, those accompanying Captain Pierson being Captain Alger, M.C., U.S.A., who was assigned to the Squadron as medical officer at the Embarkation Camp, and Lieutenant Carver, as adjutant. The other officers were detached, and sailed the same day, April 20, Easter Sunday, on board the U.S.S. *Susquehanna.*

The voyage was very uneventful, especially compared to the ex-

Cuisy (Argonne-Meuse Sector)

citement of the trip across, when submarines were a constant menace, and the men passed the time in reading and sleeping. The only excitement was when a porpoise jumped alongside the steamer, or when another steamer was sighted, which occurred but seldom. The weather was unusually good, only one storm, of two days' duration, being encountered.

Land was finally sighted at 5 a.m.. May 3, and we docked in Hoboken at 10 a.m., after a voyage of thirteen days.

Pie and coffee were served on the dock, after which the ferry took us to a Long Island train, from which we unloaded near Camp Mills. A brief march brought us to camp, where we were assigned to barracks.

At midnight the Squadron made the acquaintance of the American variety of delouser, and blouses suffered severely from the wet steam.

May 4, at 8 a.m., the Squadron marched over to Field No. 2, Garden City, and the work of demobilization was begun.

At this stage the 90th lost the services of Sergeants Hankins and Byrth, who became ill.

Captain Alger and the Medical Detachment were detached and assigned to duty with the Camp Hospital. A few days later Sergeant-Major Greer, M.E.A.S., who had also been with the Squadron from the beginning, became ill, and was transferred to the hospital for treatment, M.E.A.S. Rich replacing him.

Sergeant Greer had earned his grade after starting as a private, his work in the office being of so high a grade as to win constant recognition and steady advancement, and it was greatly regretted that he had to leave during the pressing work of demobilization. Sergeant Rich, who took his place, proved equal to the occasion, and earned special commendation for his efficient service.

After two weeks of paper work, it was finally completed, and orders received sending the men to the various discharge camps throughout the country.

The time was passed by the men in New York City for the most part, as no passes were needed to leave camp, and the men were not slow to avail themselves of the opportunity afforded.

The last detachments entrained May 22, and Captain Pierson and Lieutenant Carver received their orders relieving them from duty with the 90th.

There remained of the Squadron but the three Regular Army men, headed by Sergeant Richardson, who were to form the nucleus of the new 90th, as the name is to be preserved, and vested in a Regular

Army Squadron, to commemorate the work of the 90th in France.

As Lieutenant Looney, the old supply officer, had just arrived in camp, he was assigned to take the 90th to Kelley Field, where it arrived May 25, after having been absent, in service, for nearly two years.

Special mention should be made of the work of Supply Sergeant Jones, and Sergeants Hankins, Blake, Johnston, York, Chew, Louis Hill, and Sill. To do real justice, in fact, the Squadron roster might be cited, for all did their duty, with a will that made the 90th the success it was.

Since the St. Mihiel drive the 90th has been called a "Shock Squadron." For almost two months, without any relaxation, it carried on the difficult part assigned to Divisional Squadrons in offensive and open warfare. During that time missions were carried out in all kinds of weather, good and bad, but usually bad, and the results accomplished, as seen from the Observers' reports and the many letters of commendation and appreciation received from the divisions for which it was working, were of the utmost value to these units. The 90th has a right to feel that its work will be put on record and that the "Red Dice " will long be remembered. Our only regrets come from the loss of our four comrades who died while serving the universal cause with us, as well as of our friend, who, after bearing his part courageously and cheerfully throughout the five months which the Squadron spent on the front, was destined never to return to the United States. Compared to many other Squadrons, our list of casualties has been small, but the memory of those with whom we worked who made the supreme sacrifice from our midst, will live with us forever.

SALMSON

Memorable Incidents

The greatest danger to the 90th, In spite of their large number of combats, came not from enemy planes, but from the enemy on the ground, and from bad weather conditions. It is impossible to mention individually all the difficult missions accomplished. A few types only are picked out to illustrate.

On October 8, the 33rd Division, attached to the 17th French Army Corps, was advancing east of Consenvoye. Lieutenants Pike and Parr volunteered to find the front line. It was raining and hailing as they took off, but in the midst of this storm they flew for over an hour at fifty metres from the ground, passing through the friendly barrage and hostile machine gun fire, and brought back the desired information.

On October 13, 1918, at about 10:30 p.m., the 90th received a telephone message from G2 that it was reported that an armistice had been signed, but that no order had yet been issued to suspend hostilities. The Squadron celebrated the news in a fitting manner. Next morning an advance was scheduled to take place northwest of Cunel. The weather was so foggy that no plane was able to ascend until about noon, when Lieutenants Carver and Lindstrom decided to go up if possible and see whether the war was really over or not. On reaching the vicinity of Brieulles the weather was found to be fairly clear, and they started to stake the lines. While flying at about fifty metres from the ground the gas tank was pierced by a bullet, which first carried away the speaking tube, but the Salmson's rubber covered gas tank made it possible to drop messages to the 5th Division at Montfaucon and to the 3rd Corps at Rampont, and to land on the field at Souilly before all the gas had leaked out. It was decided that if the war was over, the Boches in the Bois de Foret had not yet been notified of the fact.

On October 21 the 3rd Corps commander sent an urgent request for a plane to ascertain whether preparations were being made by the

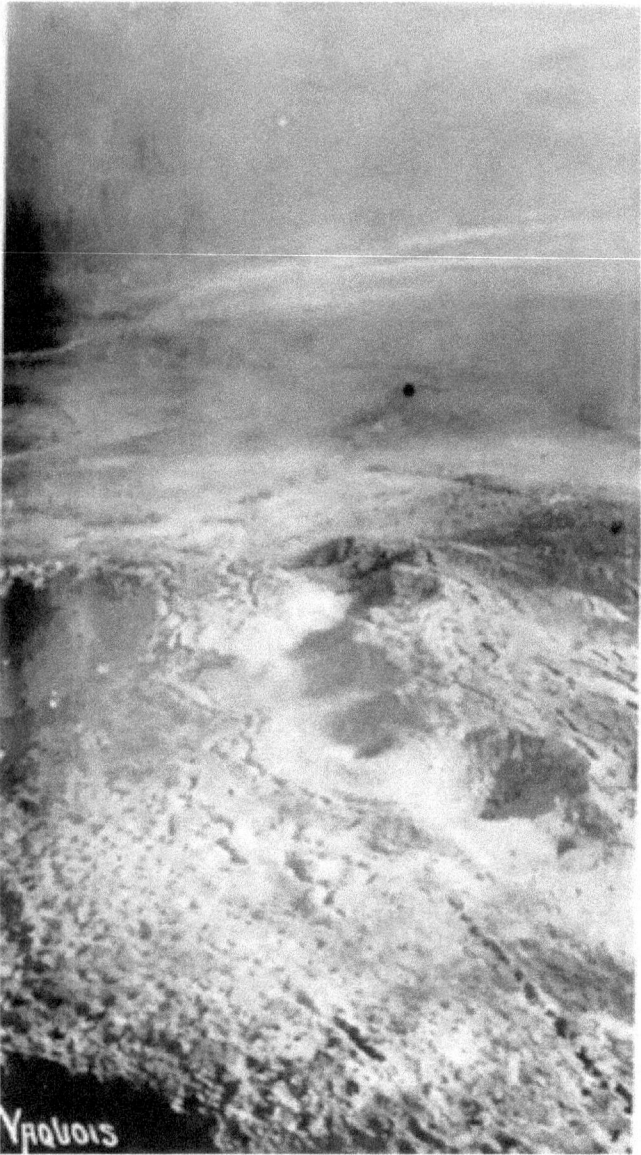

WHERE VAQUOIS WAS (ARGONNE-MEUSE SECTOR)

enemy to counterattack. Lieutenants Broomfield and Cutter volunteered. They were seen to cross the lines at about fifty metres altitude, flying in irregular course to dodge machine gun fire. A balloon observer saw them disappear for a few minutes, then reappear at about the same altitude. At 11:15 o'clock he saw the plane suddenly lurch and crash out of control the short distance to the ground. It fell in "No Man's Land," near Cote 299, northeast of Cunel, and both pilot and observer were killed instantly. As our lines advanced, both their remains and the ruins of the plane were found and identified.

On October 28, Lieutenants Conover and Burger went out on a very difficult infantry contact mission over Hill 360, east of the Meuse. Visibility was bad, and they were forced to fly at fifty metres, as the infantry were too busy to put out their panels. They detected six enemy machine gun nests which seemed to be holding up the American advance, and dived at them repeatedly, firing several hundred rounds of ammunition. Four of these machine gun nests were abandoned and the other two silenced. In the course of this action the plane was riddled with bullets, and Lieutenant Conover was wounded twice, two of the bullets tearing a large hole in his right knee. He succeeded, however, in effecting a safe landing near Consenvoye, and Lieutenant Burger immediately telephoned in his information.

Lieutenants Greist and Borden had a very exciting trip together. They went up late in the afternoon on an infantry contact mission and were attacked by three Fokkers. These they drove off, but in the delay it had become almost dark. They staked the lines and were about to return home when a six-star rocket exploded in the plane, which immediately took fire. Lieutenant Greist headed for the ground, but Lieutenant Borden grasped the flaming rocket in his hand and threw it from the plane. Then with the Pyrene can he extinguished the blaze in the fuselage and shouted to his pilot that they could return to the field, where Lieutenant Greist made a safe landing by flares.

On October 31, Lieutenants Bovard and Foster were on a reconnaissance of the enemy lines north of Aincreville, flying at about 100 metres, when they found themselves over several hostile strong points. A single gun opened on them and they retired behind our lines with a few bullet holes. Uncertain, however, whether it was a friendly or hostile gun which had fired, they entered once more and this time were fired on from all sides by every gun within range. The only direction clear was directly away from home, so the plane was forced to proceed several kilometres into hostile territory before it could swing around

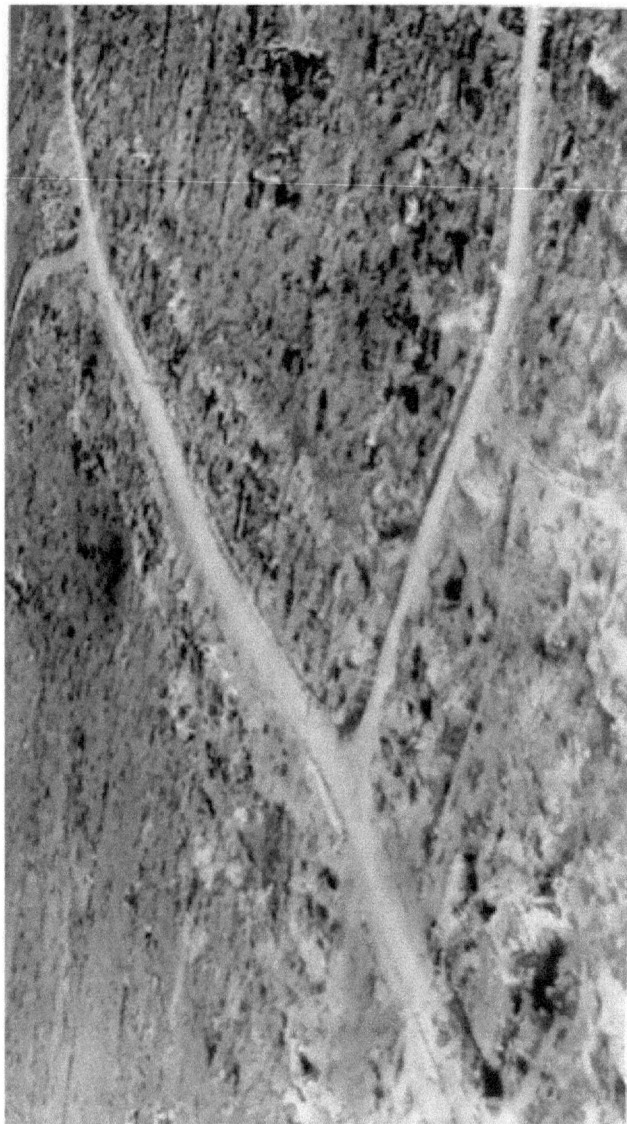

MALINCOURT (ARGONNE-MEUSE SECTOR)

the dangerous spot and retire. The engine was irreparably injured by bullets in the radiator and oiling system, but completed the trip back to the field before giving out entirely.

Lieutenants Neidecker and Lake, on November 3, flew a general reconnaissance for the 17th French Corps. They penetrated the enemy lines so far that they went entirely off their map, but flying at 200 metres they picked up much information which they were able to locate on the map after their return. At one point they saw a train of nineteen cars moving along a siding, filled with troops. They dived and raked the whole length of it with machine gun bullets.

On the morning of November 1 the main offensive was renewed west of the Meuse. A thick mist and light rain made it seemingly impossible for a plane to take off without danger of crashing. It was of utmost importance, however, that the location of our lines be ascertained. Lieutenants Greist and Burger volunteered for this mission. When they took off, the fog was so thick that they were forced to just skim the ground, relying on their intimate knowledge of the sector to find their way to the lines. They ran the risk of running into hills in their blindness, and were almost constantly in their own barrage. Without any protection they penetrated five kilometres behind the German lines, and returned with valuable information as to the disposition of the enemy artillery and infantry. They flew along the barrage lines just over the heads of our infantry so that Lieutenant Burger could stake our lines. The ship was so tossed about by the concussion of bursting shells underneath that both pilot and observer were made very sick. Finishing their mission successfully, they landed at an aerodrome, delivered their information, and set off once more in the fog for home. This was the only mission carried out over the sector that day, and brought the divisional commander the only information he received as to the location of his front lines, and all the information was later verified.

Both Lieutenant Greist and Lieutenant Burger were recommended for the Medal of Honour for extraordinary heroism.

The following military decorations have been conferred on officers of the 90th Aero Squadron:

DISTINGUISHED SERVICE CROSS

Second Lieut. Valentine J. Berger (with oak leaf).
First Lieut. Harvey Conover.
First Lieut. E. Harold Greist.

First Lieut. Wilbert E. Kinsley.

First Lieut. William O. Lowe.

Second Lieut. Fred A. Tillman.

LEGION OF HONOUR

Second Lieut. Fred A. Tillman.

CROIX DE GUERRE

First Lieut. Morton B. Adams.

Second Lieut. Valentine J. Burger (with palm).

First Lieut. Harvey Conover.

Second Lieut. Alexander Grier.

Second Lieut. Horace A. Lake (with palm).

Maj. William G. Schauffler, Jr.

Second Lieut. Fred A. Tillman (with palm).

AERO CLUB OF AMERICA MEDAL OF HONOUR

First Lieut. Harvey Conover.

Seven Up

In the choice of an insignia the Squadron was fortunate. It is a rule of the Air Service that no squadron shall have an insignia until it has seen three months' service at the Front. The time for the 90th to adopt one came while it was stationed at Ourches. There was a frenzied fortnight of verbal strife between parties supporting different designs. No one is quite clear as to the reasons which led to the triumph of the dice. Some claim that it was through the influence of certain members who through this symbol cornered the money market after every pay day.

Whatever the cause, this insignia, first used by Captain Schauffler while with the First Aero Squadron, became the emblem of the 90th, and in short order all the planes of the Squadron blossomed out with red dice twelve by twelve, with white eyes. Whatever way the dice are read they come "Seven." That this was a lucky emblem the multitude of successful missions and seven official victories In the air, prove. Other Squadrons cried for replacements, but the dice of the 90th brought her veterans through with but very few casualties, only one plane being lost over the lines, which is probably a unique record among Squadrons which saw an equal period of service at the front.

Combat Reports—Confirmations

The first question an aviator asks of any old acquaintance whom he has not seen for some time is, "Get any Boches lately?" This shows the tendency to give great importance in aerial work to combats, to getting a "Hun." In the case of Observation Squadrons this emphasis is wrongly placed, since the measure of success of such a squadron is measured not in terms of combats but in terms of accurate information brought back and this means dodging battles instead of seeking them. None the less, accuracy with a machine gun is an essential accomplishment both for pilots and observers and a good record against the Fokkers is certainly something to be proud of.

In its five months on the front the 90th engaged in over twenty-five aerial battles, practically all of which were in the last two months, as it was very rare to see a Boche plane in the St. Mihiel sector before the drive of September 12. As a result of these combats the Squadron was credited officially with the destruction of seven enemy planes, in addition to which several others were in fact brought down, and in all these combats lost but one plane, which may have been brought down from the ground. The records which follow give some idea of the odds at which our men always fought and of one part of the danger which awaited them on a large proportion of their missions. On September 20, 1918, Lieutenant Hart, Pilot, and Lieutenant Grier, Observer, while acting as protection for another observation plane, were engaged in the following combat west of Dampvitoux in the St. Mihiel sector at 17:44 o'clock.

While flying above in the rear of the observation plane, Lieutenant Grier sighted a single enemy plane flying below him, within the German lines, and at an altitude of about 200 metres. The Boche did not attack, but manoeuvred suspiciously to attract attention. Expecting a ruse of some sort, Lieutenant Grier began to watch the sky above him, especially a white puff of cloud within the enemy lines, at the same time moving his guns into a position ready to meet an attack from that direction. They were flying at about 800 metres, when suddenly three Fokkers shot out from the cloud at an altitude of about 1000 metres and dived to attack from the rear, firing as they came.

Lieutenant Grier held his fire until he had a good range and then opened up on the leader. He saw his tracer bullets hit the enemy plane in several places, and then saw the plane go into a vertical dive with smoke pouring from the motor and fuselage. He watched it fall until a second Fokker came down upon him, which he succeeded in driving off with sixty or seventy well-directed shots from his Lewis gun. The enemy craft then gave up the fight and disappeared among the clouds behind their own lines. The plane, in which were Lieutenants Grier and Hart, also bore several marks of battle. Wings, tail and fuselage were punctured by bullets, several having passed within a few inches of the observer, and one severing a brace wire on the rudder.

Order of Confirmation.

Headquarters Air Service, First Army
American Expeditionary Force
France, September 27, 1918.

General Orders
No. 10

Extract

2. Second Lieut. F. H. Hart, Pilot, and A. T. Grier, Observer, 90th Aero Squadron, 3rd Corps Observation Group, are hereby credited with the destruction in combat of an enemy airplane in the region of Dampvitoux at 800 metres altitude, on September 20, 1918, at 17:45 o'clock.

By Order of Colonel Mitchell,
T. DeW. Milling,
Col., A.S. U.S.A., Chief of Staff.

Official:
M. P. Kelleher, Major.

Lieut. W. G. Schauffler, pilot, and Lieut. Morton B. Adams, observer, while dropping newspapers to our troops along the southern edge of the Bois de Dannevoux, on October 1, 1918, were attacked by eight Fokker chasse planes at an altitude of 500 metres. The Hun, employing his usual method of attack, came down from the rear on their tail, firing as they dived. The third plane to attack succeeded in cutting away the horns on the right elevator, thus rendering the right elevator control wire useless. Lieutenant Adams in the meantime had been pouring a stream of bullets into the second, third and fourth enemy planes as they came down on him in quick succession. It was on the fourth Boche that his bullets took vital effect. This plane was seen to issue a great cloud of black smoke, turn sharply to the right, and start rapidly towards the earth and in the direction of the German lines.

As he watched for an instant the downward course of the enemy looked more and more as if the Fokker were in flames and out of control. The remaining four planes overhead claimed his attention by their manoeuvring but did not attack again, even when Lieutenant Schauffler turned his plane toward the German lines. During this fight Lieutenant Adams observed a new type of German *cocarde*. One of the Hun machines bore, instead of the customary black Maltese cross, a circle on the wings in which a very small cross was painted.

Order of Confirmation.

Headquarters Air Service, First Army
American Expeditionary Force
France, October 23, 1918.

General Orders
No. 20.

Extract

13. First Lieuts. W. G. Schauffler, Jr., and Morton B. Adams, 90th Aero Squadron, 3rd Observation Group, are hereby credited with the destruction in combat of an enemy Fokker in the region of Dannevoux, at 500 metres altitude, on October 1, 1918, at 5 :00 o'clock (p.m.).

By Order of Colonel Milling.

W. C. Sherman,
Lieut. Col., A.S. U.S.A., Chief of Staff.

Official:
H. S. Sturgis,
Second Lieut., A.S. U.S.A., Adjutant.

Lieut. W. E. Kinsley, pilot, and Lieut. W. O. Lowe, observer, while on an infantry liaison mission in the vicinity of Cunel, on October 7, 1918, at an altitude of 300 to 600 metres, sighted eight hostile planes north of Cunel. They watched these planes until they disappeared, and then approached the southern end of the Bois du Foret, where Lieutenant Lowe called for our lines by Very pistol signals. They then turned south and crossed the Cunel-Brieulles road, where they were attacked by the eight Fokkers previously seen, which dived suddenly from a cloud over their right wing.

Two Germans opened fire immediately at a range of 150 metres and came into thirty metres. Lieutenant Lowe opened fire on the first one, directing tracers into the motor, which caused the Boche to stop firing immediately. Lieutenant Lowe then turned his guns on the second plane, which was only about 75 metres away, and which approached to within thirty-five metres of the Salmson's tail, when he viraged off, exposing his entire lower side. Lieutenant Lowe took advantage of the opportunity and, firing a quick burst, saw several tracers enter the fuselage under the pilot's seat.

The result was quickly seen, for the Hun started to fall, out of control. At this moment the first plane to attack was seen to hit the ground in a vertical nose dive at point 11.7-85.4, just east of Cunel. Two more planes followed up the attack of their fallen leaders, both firing at the same time, but from the respectful range of 300 metres. Lieutenant Lowe then engaged the nearest of them and directed several tracers into the fuselage, whereupon they withdrew and rejoined the remnants of their formation. Two more planes still higher manoeuvred for position, but were unsuccessful and did not attack.

This first incident over, Lieutenant Kinsley withdrew a short distance into friendly territory and watched the enemy out of sight. Then they returned to their mission, but were immediately pounced upon by six hostile scouts, who manoeuvred to attack from their right rear. Lieutenant Lowe opened fire at 400 metres, but seeing that they were watched, the enemy withdrew to the north.

The effect of the Boche machine gun fire was not serious. One bullet had punctured the rudder, three had passed through the right elevator, and one through the left elevator.

Order of Confirmation.

Headquarters Air Service, First Army
American Expeditionary Force
France, October 23, 1918.

General Order
No. 20.

Extract

18. Second Lieuts. W. E. Kinsley and W. O. Lowe, 90th Aero Squadron, 3rd Observation Group, are hereby credited with the

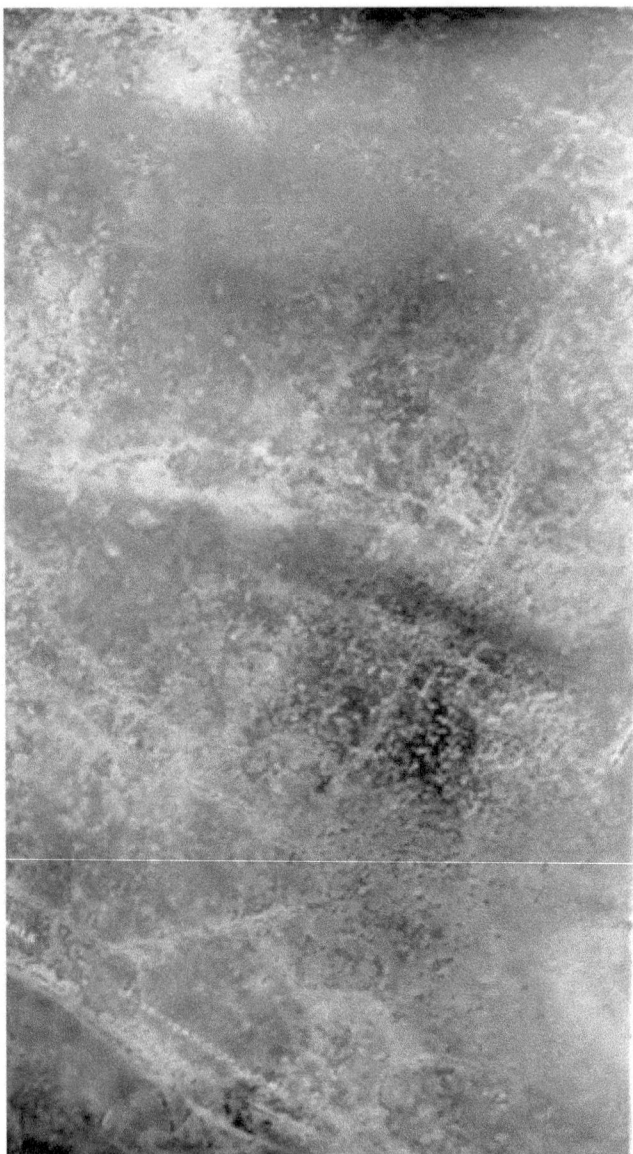

"Dead Man's Hill" (Meuse Sector)

destruction, in combat, of an enemy Fokker, in the region of Cunel, at 400 metres altitude, on October 7, 1918, at 12:30 o'clock.

By Order of Colonel Milling.

W. C. Sherman,
Lieut. Col., A.S. U.S.A., Chief of Staff.

Official:

H. S. Sturgis,
Second Lieut., A.S. U.S.A., Adjutant.

Lieut. Harvey Conover, pilot, and Lieut. V. J. Burger, observer, while engaged in a dangerous Infantry contact mission with the 17th French Army Corps, east of the Meuse, near Sivry, on October 10, 1918, were attacked three times during the same flight by enemy chasse patrols. The first, a patrol of five, attacked vigorously, and only by clever manoeuvring was Lieutenant Conover able to keep his plane so placed that Lieutenant Burger could fire effectively. The result of this first attack, however, was the crashing of one plane and the driving off of the remaining four. Returning then to their mission, they were again attacked on two different occasions, but by good flying and good shooting in a running fight, they were able to hold the enemy off and complete an important mission.

The American plane, after this series of combats, was riddled with bullets, wires were cut, spars split, and ribs damaged. In fact, so many parts were broken or damaged that the plane was declared unsafe for further flying and had to be salvaged. Bullets had also passed through Lieutenant Burger's flying suit, but no injury had been done to pilot or observer.

Order of Confirmation.

Headquarters Air Service, First Army
American Expeditionary Force
France, October 23, 1918.

General Order
No. 20.

Extract

29. First Lieut. Harvey Conover and Second Lieut. V. J. Burger, 90th Aero Squadron, 3rd Corps Observation Group, are hereby credited with the destruction, in combat, of an enemy Fokker, in the region of Sivry sur Meuse, at 500 metres altitude, on October 10, 1918, 16:45 o'clock.

By Order of Colonel Milling.

W. C. Sherman,

Lieut. Col, A.S. U.S.A., Chief of Staff.

Official:

H. S. Sturgis,

Second Lieut., A.S. U.S.A., Adjutant.

On October 22, 1918, Lieut. B. C. Neidecker, pilot, and Lieut. Horace Lake, observer, were sent across the lines to drop a note concerning the whereabouts of Lieutenants Broomfield and Cutter, who had been missing since undertaking a dangerous mission the preceding day. At 15:15 o'clock, at 1000 metres over Clery-le-Grand, and when just in the act of dropping the message container, they were attacked by seven Boche planes. The first dived straight on their tail, using the unmistakable incendiary bullets. Lieutenant Lake opened fire immediately and succeeded in sending the machine down in a *vrille* with smoke pouring from the fuselage.

A second Fokker dived immediately and *viraged* off at a distance of about 100 metres. At that moment both of Lieutenant Lake's magazines were empty and, as a third Fokker was attacking, he called to Lieutenant Neidecker, who immediately put his plane in a straight nose dive, followed by the German, who was shooting as he came. During the dive. Lieutenant Lake replaced his empty magazines, and when Lieutenant Neidecker straightened out, opened fire at his pursuer. Immediately the fire was opened the Fokker turned off and flew back into his own lines.

The entire fight lasted four minutes, and this plane was the only allied plane over the sector at the time.

Order of Confirmation.

Headquarters Air Service, First Army

American Expeditionary Force

France, November 2, 1918.

General Order

No. 22.

Extract

8. First Lieutenant B. C. Neidecker and Second Lieut. H. A. Lake, 90th Aero Squadron, 3rd Observation Group, are hereby credited with the destruction, in combat, of an enemy Fokker, in the region north of the Bois de Foret, west of Clery, at 1000 metres altitude, October 22, 1918, 3:40 p.m.

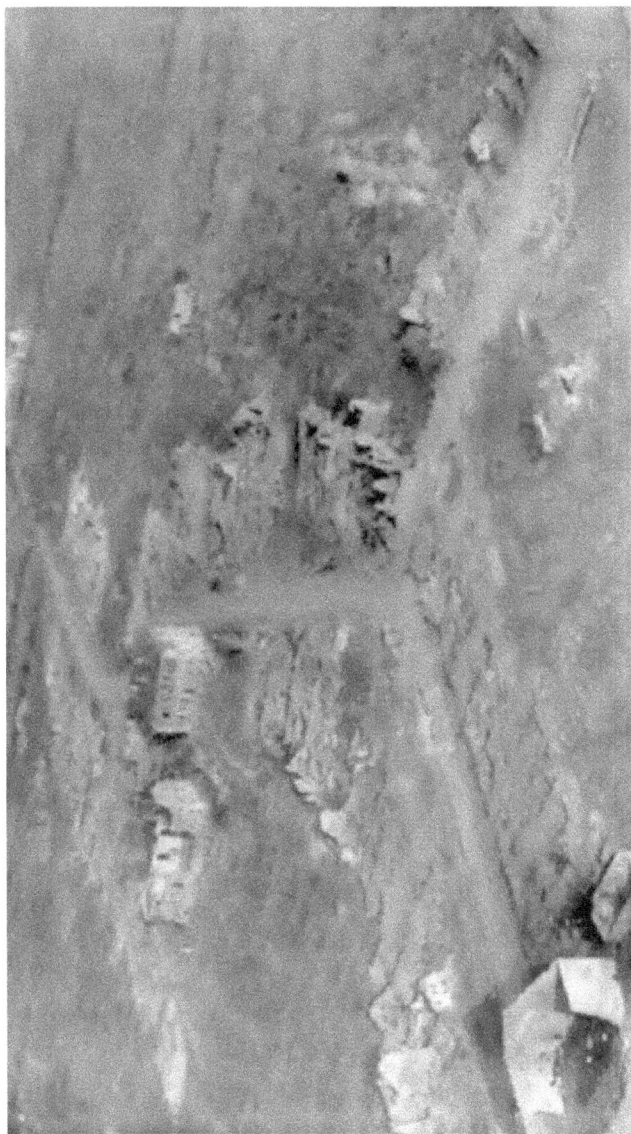

SEPTSARGES, (ARGONNE-MEUSE SECTOR)

By Order of Colonel Milling.

W. C. Sherman,

Lieut. Col., Chief of Staff.

Official

H. S. Sturgis,

Second Lieut., Adjutant.

On November 4, 1918, while performing an infantry contact mission, Lieut. L. E. Rohrer, pilot, and Lieut. A. T. Foster, observer, in one plane, and Lieut. W. E. Kinsley, Pilot, with Lieut. L. M. Hall, Observer, in another plane as protection, were attacked by seven Fokkers. Four enemy planes singled out Lieutenants Rohrer and Foster, while the other three concentrated on Lieutenants Kinsley and Hall. It was about 15:35 o'clock and both observation planes were flying at about 300 metres. Lieutenant Foster and his pilot saw the scouts just as they approached the Foret de Dienlet, high overhead, and turned south. As they turned, the Boche split their formation and came down to attack both planes.

Three of the enemy, attacking Lieutenant Rohrer, came down on his tail to within 100 metres, Lieutenant Foster in the meantime firing about eighty rounds from each gun. The leader dropped suddenly and disappeared from sight behind a wing, going down out of control. The two following did not approach so closely, but fired a considerable number of rounds and then turned off. Lieutenants Rohrer and Foster then made another attempt to find the lines, but were met by two Fokkers, with whom they exchanged shots with no apparent effects. Returning for the third time to try for the lines they were met by nine Fokkers, attacking from above and to the left.

Unfortunately, Lieutenant Foster's guns jammed after a few rounds and it was necessary for them to try and get away. The enemy planes followed them for about a kilometre and forced them down to within about 100 metres of the ground before the observer's guns were in action again and he could turn them off with his fire. Lieutenant Rohrer then attempted to go home, but two more Huns arrived and forced them several kilometres west of Montfaucon, in a running fight, while his observer continued to keep tracers sufficiently close to the enemy pilots to prevent their closing in on them.

Order of Confirmation.

Headquarters Air Service, First Army

American Expeditionary Force

Montfaucon (Argonne-Meuse Sector)

France, November 19, 1918.

General Orders
No. 28.

Extract

33. First Lieuts. L. E. Rohrer and A. T. Foster, 90th Aero Squadron, 3rd Observation Group, are hereby credited with the destruction, in combat, of an enemy Fokker, in the region of Foret de Dienlet, at 300 metres altitude, on November 4, 1918, at 14:10 o'clock.

By Order of Colonel Milling.

W. C. Sherman,
Lieut. Col., G.S. U.S.A., Chief of Staff.

Official:

H. S. Sturgis,
First Lieut., A.S., Adjutant.

Lieuts. John S. Young and V. J. Burger, while on a reconnaissance of the 90th Division sector on November 3, 1918, had the following interesting combat with a single enemy Fokker over Stenay, at 15:30 o'clock. They arrived over Stenay at an altitude of 300 metres and saw four hostile planes, which circled back into the German lines while they turned south toward their own. Three times they flew over the town of Stenay, and each time were chased away by the four Boches, who did not fire a shot but seemed content to chase only. On the fourth trip over the town they were attacked vigorously by a single Fokker of the latest type—D VII.

The Boche was a daring flyer and an excellent shot. His endeavors to get under their tail and to turn them back into the German lines were unsuccessful, however. Finally he resorted to the old diving method, and approached to within twenty metres on their left side. In *viraging* off he exposed his entire under side for an instant and then It was that Lieutenant Burger filled his motor, body, wings, and the under side of the fuselage with both tracer and ordinary bullets. The German's manoeuvre was fatal to him, and he fell off in a slow loose *vrllle* toward the ground.

The statement that the Boche was an excellent shot was borne out by an examination of the American plane after landing. Six bullets had pierced the right wing, two had punctured the gas tank, six had gone through the tall, one had split the propeller, and one put out the wireless generator. One bullet had passed through Lieutenant Burger's combination suit, just missing his leg.

Interest was added to this combat by the fact that the Boche pilot bore on his plane five vertical white stripes, proclaiming him five times an ace. His excellent ability as a flier and his accurate shooting might well bear out the evidence.

Order of Confirmation.

Headquarters Air Service, First Army

American Expeditionary Force

France, November 17, 1918.

Special Orders
No. 27.

Extract

18. First Lieut. John S. Young and Second Lieut. V. J. Burger, 90th Aero Squadron, 3rd Observation Group, are hereby credited with the destruction, in combat, of an enemy Fokker in the region south of Stenay, at 300 metres altitude, on November 3, 1918, at 16:35 o'clock.

By Order of Colonel Milling.

W. C. Sherman,

Lieut. Col., G.S. U.S.A.

Official:

H. S. Sturgis,

First Lieut., AS. U.S.A., Adjutant.

Other Combats of the 90th Aero Squadron

Lieutenants M. O. White and J. C. Sherrick, at 11:25 o'clock on September 26, 1918, while on a surveillance mission over Bois de Forges, at 300 metres, were engaged in combat with six Fokker scouts. Their plane was untouched and none of their shots seemed to take effect on the enemy.

Lieuts. John Livingston and Pressley B. Shuss, while on an infantry liaison mission over Sivry sur Meuse, on September 26, 1918, at 150 metres altitude, were met by six Fokker scouts. The enemy did not succeed in getting into position to attack. Lieutenant Shuss' fire appeared to be very accurate but he did not succeed in bringing the enemy down.

Lieuts. W. B. Schauffler, Jr., and Fred A. Tillman, while on a reconnaissance from Forges to Dannevoux, on September 26, 1918, at 300 metres altitude, met a patrol of twelve enemy scouts. Five manoeuvred for position but only one attacked, which Lieutenant Schauffler drove off with fire from his forward gun. No hits were made by either pilot.

On September 28, 1918, Lieuts. H. R. Ellis and H. L. Borden, while flying over Brieulles, on a reconnaissance mission, at an altitude of 250 metres, met six Fokker scouts. Inviting combat several times, they were finally attacked from two sides but drove the enemy off by well-directed machine gun fire. Time, 12:50 o'clock.

While performing a reconnaissance mission on September 29, 1918, 300 metres over the Bois de Forges, Lieut. F. H. Hart, Pilot, and Lieut. A. T. Grier, Observer, were fired upon by a Breguet, presumably flown by the enemy. The fire was returned without result. Time, 7:00 o'clock.

Lieut. Leland M. Carver, pilot, and Lieut. Gustaf T. Lindstrom, observer, while flying over the Bois de Cote Lemont at an altitude of

CLOUDS FROM THE AIR (ST. MIHIEL SECTOR)
"TILL THE BOCHES FLY THE HEAVENS NO MORE"
SOUTHEAST OF BRIEULLES

500 metres, at 7:23 o'clock, October 2, 1918, engaged in a running fight with two groups of enemy scouts. Five planes attacked in the first group and four in the second. Apparently no shots took effect from either side.

Lieut. John Livingston, Pilot, and Lieut. H. L. Borden, Observer, while about to commence an artillery *reglage* on a hostile battery in the Bois de Chaume, at 11:40 o'clock, October 3, 1918, in company with two protection planes, were attacked at 800 metres altitude by nine enemy Fokkers. The Boche dived on the formation from the clouds. Lieutenant Borden opened a hot fire on the attacking planes with apparently good results. His plane suffered no damage.

Lieut. H. H. Cowle, pilot, and Lieut. Walter Frances, observer, while acting as protection for the above *reglage* plane, took part in the same fight. Lieutenant Frances fired over 200 rounds at the enemy, several tracers taking effect in the wings and fuselage of the hostile planes. One enemy plane was seen to fall, but recovered after falling 50 metres. The American plane was not damaged.

Lieut. Loren Rohrer, pilot, with Lieutenant Vinson, observer, also took part in the above engagement. Lieutenants Rohrer and Vinson, being the rear plane in the formation, were the principal targets of the enemy. Lieutenant Vinson fired 100 rounds from his guns with apparently good effect, and saw several bullets hit the enemy. He saw one plane start to fall, but had no time to watch it down. His plane was riddled with bullets, brace wires cut, and the upper wing set on fire by incendiary bullets.

Flying over Bois de Lartelle, on a reconnaissance mission, at 9:00 o'clock on October 5, 1918, at 800 metres altitude, Lieut. Norris E. Pierson, pilot, and Lieut. Van B. Hayden, observer, engaged five enemy Fokkers in a running fight. About thirty-five rounds were fired by Lieutenant Hayden without apparent effect. Due to the fine speed and manoeuvring ability of the Salmson, the Boches could not get into a good attacking position.

Lieutenants Pierson and Hayden, at 9:20 o'clock, on October 10, 1918, while flying on an infantry contact mission over Cunel, met four Fokkers, who dived and opened fire. Some of our Spads then put the enemy to flight.

While flying over Fountaine at 7:05 o'clock, October 21, 1918, and performing an infantry contact mission at 300 metres altitude. Lieutenant Hart, pilot, and Lieutenant Grier, observer, engaged in combat with an enemy Rumpler biplane, which was apparently out to locate the Boche front line. After making several attacks upon the Rumpler, they succeeded in forcing him to quit his mission and to leave the vicinity.

Lieut. W. E. Kinsley, pilot, and Lieut. A. E. Parr, observer, while on a special reconnaissance to Villers devant Dun, at 13:20 o'clock, on the 29th of October, 1918, at 300 metres altitude, were attacked by two Fokker scouts. Beating them off with machine gun fire, the Americans turned and gave chase, following the Boches to Aincreville, firing as often as possible. The enemy fire shattered one strut and broke a spar in the aileron of the lower right wing. One of the enemy was seen to be hit, but not out of control. Flying as protection for another observation plane, Lieut. W. E. Kinsley, pilot, and Lieut. L. M. Hall, observer, while flying over the Font de Dienlle at 600 metres altitude on November 4, 1918, were attacked by five enemy scouts. The enemy fire was very poor, but Lieutenant Hall by good shooting forced the enemy to turn off and retire. Time, 14:15 o'clock.

Lieut. E. H. Greist, pilot, and Lieutenant Borden, observer, while returning from a reconnaissance mission in the vicinity of Brandville at 12:48 o'clock on November 4, 1918, at 500 metres altitude, were being heavily archied when they were suddenly attacked by a single black Fokker, who got a position on their tail. Lieutenant Borden opened fire at the Boche as he dived and saw his bullets entering the fuselage and passing all around the enemy plane. Three times the Fokker attacked, but the last two times he veered off as Lieutenant Borden's tracers began to flash by him. The Salmson suffered considerable damage, fifteen bullets having passed through the plane, piercing the oil tank, wings and fuselage.

While on a reconnaissance mission near Fontaine at 11:10 o'clock on November 6, 1918, Lieut. Marshall G. Lee, pilot, and Lieut. H. W. Phillips, observer, were attacked by a group of four Fokkers, one plane leaving the formation to attack them. Lieutenant Phillips opened fire, and the Boche at once turned away and returned to his own lines. No damage was done to the Salmson.

SOPWITH

71

Ninetieth Songs

During the stay of the Ninetieth across the big pond experience was gained in many lines of activity. Many composers, soloists, and mixers of rare harmony were developed. Many of the long evenings were passed in song about the mess table after Corn Willy and his *cohorts* had been vanquished. The words to most of the songs were written by members of the Ninetieth and the tunes used were confiscated from all sources as a wartime necessity. It would take a volume to print them all, so only the most popular ones have been inserted here.

> *Happy Landings, Ninetieth!*
> *(Tune: "Alma Mater," Cornell)*
> *Flying low o'er Verdun's trenches,*
> *'Midst the shot and shell,*
> *A pair of dice our lucky emblem.*
> *Give the Huns more hell.*
>
> *Chorus*
> *Tails up and flying any weather,*
> *Where'er the call may be,*
> *Happy landings, Ninetieth Squadron,*
> *Hail, all hail to thee!*
>
> *Far above the noise of battle,*
> *Dodging Archies' fire.*
> *Taking photos far in Hunland,*
> *That's our heart's desire! (Shout LIKE HELL!)*
>
> *Ninetieth ties can ne'er be broken,*
> *Wherever we may fly,*
> *Friendships formed in face of danger,*
> *They can never die.*
>
> *Where'er the coming years may find us,*

Whate'er the fates prevail.
Memories of our comrades bind us
And we'll never fail.

THE FESTIVE AIRMEN

We're going to blind the enemy, so all the papers say;
We fly the festive Liberty, we're missing the next day;
A bullet in our gas tank, we kiss the world goodbye;
They say its for democracy, and we fall from the sky.

Chorus:
For we're the airmen, the festive airmen,
Perhaps we never should have flown, for our ships were made at home.
For we're the airmen, the festive airmen,
We invite you all to come and fly the ship called Liberty.

We are a bunch of ambusques, so all the doughboys say;
We live a life of luxury and draw our flying pay;
We fly up to their trenches, and when we're overhead,
They point their machine guns at us and fill us full of lead.
Chorus.

We like to see the regular, who has a J.M.A.,
Sit in his cosy dugout with one-half extra pay;
He tells us how to fight the war, for he shot on a sleeve.
And if we bring down all the Boche, we may get three days' leave.
Chorus.

We get into a scrap each day, six Fokkers on our tail,
We see the tracers streaming by, they shoot away our tail;
We bring old Fritzie down in flames, we see him kiss the ground;
They say for confirmation, "The Archies brought him down."
Chorus.

For we're the airmen, the festive airmen.
Perhaps we never should have flown, for our ships were made at home;
For we're the airmen, the festive airmen.
We invite you all to come and fly the ship called Liberty.

OH, THEY SAY TRUE LOVE IS A BLESSING

Oh, they say true love is a blessing.
It's a blessing I never could see,
For the only girl that I ever loved.
Has just gone back on me.

She has gone, let her go, God bless her;
She is mine where e'er she may be;
She can search this wide world over, but—
She'll have to fly like hell to catch me!

Oh, I've looked at the girls in New York,
In London and gay Paree.
And the one conclusion that I have got.
There are other little fishes in the sea.
She has gone, let her go, God bless her,
For I am far across the sea
She wanted to marry a tin soldier, but—
A Home Guard I never could be.

TODAY IS MONDAY

Today is Monday, today is Monday, Monday bullets. Oh, you dirty Germans, we wish the same to you.

Today is Tuesday, today is Tuesday, Tuesday's Archies, Monday's bullets; oh, you dirty Germans, we wish the same to you.

Today is Wednesday, today is Wednesday, Wednesday's onions, Tuesday's Archies, Monday's bullets; oh, you dirty Germans, we wish the same to you.

Today is Thursday, today is Thursday, Thursday Fokkers, Wednesday onions, Tuesday's Archies, Monday's bullets. Oh, you dirty Germans, we wish the same to you.

Today is Friday, today is Friday, Friday side-slips, Thursday's Fokkers, Wednesday's onions, Tuesday's Archies, Monday's bullets. Oh, you dirty Germans, we wish the same to you.

Today is Saturday, today is Saturday, Saturday's hospital, Friday sideslips, Thursday's Fokkers, Wednesday's onions, Tuesday's Archies, Monday's bullets. Oh, you dirty Germans, we wish the same to you.

Today is Sunday, today is Sunday, Sunday's funerals, Saturday's hospitals, Friday's side-slips, Thursday's Fokkers, Wednesday's onions, Tuesday's Archies, Monday's bullets. Oh, you dirty Germans, we wish the same to you.

OH, NINETY, BRAVE NINETY!
(Tune: "Lord Geoffrey Amherst")
Oh, the men of the Ninetieth they came across the sea,
To fight in a far country;
To the Germans and the Austrians they didn't do a thing,
In the air of this great country,

In the air of this great country;
For the honour of the Ninetieth they fought with all their might,
For they were airmen tried and true,
And they brought down all the Albatross that came within their sight.
And they straffed the German lines when they were through.

Chorus

Oh, Ninety, brave Ninety, it's a name known to fame in days of war,
May she ever be glorious, till the Boches fly the heavens no more!

I WANT TO GO HOME!

I want to go home, I want to go home;
The guerre it is fini, my francs they are too.
We're stuck in a mud hole with nothing to do.
We've finished with tempting the fates—
We want to go back to the States!
Oh, my! Who the hell wants to fly?
We want to go home!

We want to go home, we want to go home;
We've burned all our wood and can't find any more,
The wind whistles up through the cracks in the floor;
There are leaks in the barracks roof, too;
We'll all get pneumonia or "flu."
Oh my! We don't want to die,
We want to go home!

We want to go home, we want to go home;
We can't get our pay checks, we've spent all our kale,
And day after day never get any mail.
If you like this damned country, then stay!
Send me back to the old U. S A.
Oh, Oui! Old Broadway for me—
I want to go home!

ARMAMENT CREW

SUPPLY CREW

AFTER MESS

"IT WAS AN AWFUL WAR" (?)

RADIO STATION

OFFICE CREW

RADIO CREW

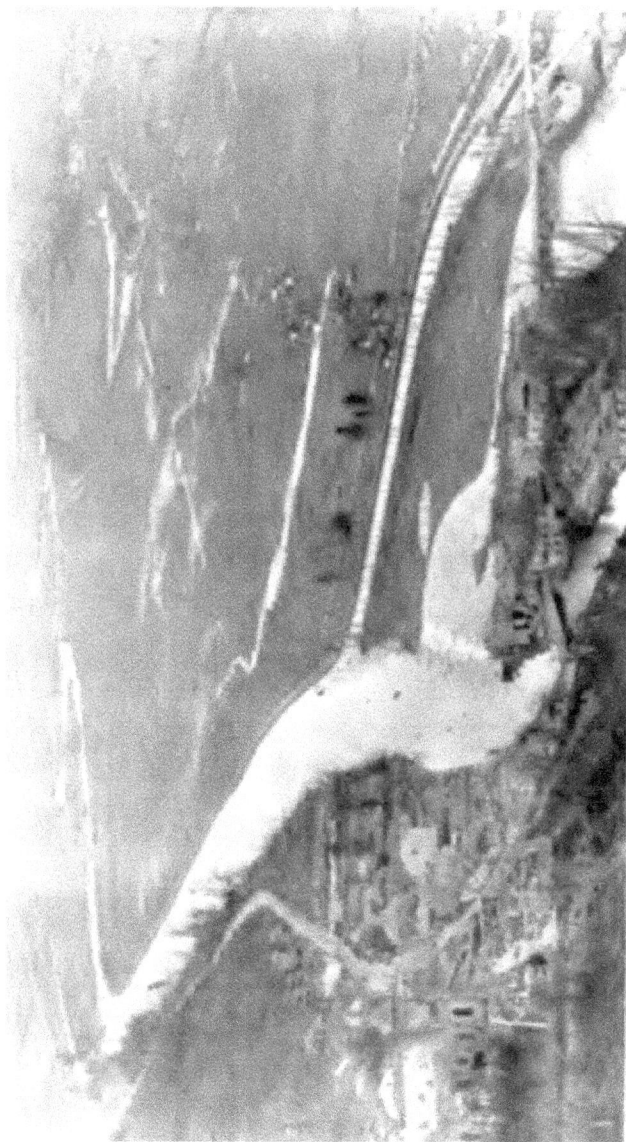

DUN-SUR-MEUSE (MEUSE SECTOR)

Personnel of Squadron

An Observation Squadron is a complex organisation, and it was found impossible to give much space in the history to the changes which this organisation underwent without making it an unwieldy and unreadable mass of detail. It was one of the causes of our success, however, that the right men filled the right places; the results accomplished by a mission over the front are as much the work of the mechanics who have kept the plane in condition to fly, as of the pilot and observer who actually perform it.

Every man in the Squadron has played a part in the game, and all have played it with an enthusiasm and pride in their work which has marked the 90th wherever it has been as a Squadron which could accomplish things.

The organisation underwent very few changes during its duty at the front, and it is probably due to this fact that there were so few casualties, as the pilots and observers of the various planes understood each other through long association, and the crews showed a very fine spirit, taking the liveliest interest in their work.

Following is the organisation of the flights at the two most important points of the Squadron's existence—St. Mihiel, and Verdun—and the rest of the enlisted personnel and roster of officers is given as at the time of the armistice:

PERSONNEL OF 90TH SQUADRON DURING ST. MIHIEL OFFENSIVE

Commanding Officer — Lieut. Schauffler, Lieut. Gallop (acting until September 15)
Adjutant — Lieut. Hackett
Operations Officer — Lieut. Adams

"A" FLIGHT

Sgt. 1st Cl. York, in charge of hangar

Pilot	Observer	Crew Chief	Assistant
1—Lt. White (Flight Commander)	Lt. Sherrick	Chf. Hunsacker	Pvt. Antosh
2—Lt. Livingston	Lt. Shuss	Chf. Auten	Pvt. 1st Cl. Pino
3—Lt. Cowle	Lt. Francis	Chf. De Baun	Pvt. 1st Cl. McWhirter
4—Lt. Conover	Lt. Burger	Chf. O'Connell	Pvt. Blackledge
5—Lt. Hart	Lt. Grier	Chf. Tiller	Pvt. 1st. Cl. Stone
6—Lt. Dorrance		Sgt. 1st Cl. Chew	Pvt. Bertonz

"B" FLIGHT

Sgt. 1st Cl. Blake, in charge of hangar

Pilot	Observer	Crew Chief	Assistant
7—Lt. Greist (Flight Commander)	Lt. Tillman	Sgt. Goodman	Pvt. 1st Cl. King
8—Lt. Neidecker	Lt. Lake	Sgt. Medlin	Pvt. 1st Cl. Buckley
9—Lt. Ellis	Lt. Borden	Chf. Grice	Cpl. Barton
10—Lt. Kinsley	Lt. Lowe	Sgt. Cargill	Pvt. 1st Cl. Killman
11—Lt. Bovard	Lt. Sullivan	Sgt. Clifton	Pvt. 1st Cl. Kendricks
12—Lt. Carver	Lt. Lindstrom	Chf. Farrand	Cpl. Bunning

"C" FLIGHT

Sgt. 1st Cl. Johnson, in charge of hangar

Pilot	Observer	Crew Chief	Assistant
13—Lt. Pierson (Flight Commander)	Lt. Haydon	Chf. 1st Cl. Richey	Cpl. Carson
14—Lt. Lee	Lt. Waldon	Sgt. Jaeger	Pvt. Larson
15—Lt. Rohrer	Lt. Vinson	Chf. Pheiffer	Pvt. Lackey
16—Lt. Pike	Lt. Parr	Sgt. 1st Cl. Ford	Pvt. De Young
17—Lt. Gallup		Sgt. 1st Cl. Van Sickle	Pvt. Brickey
18—Lt. Young	Lt. Bogle	Sgt. Bair	Cpl. Morrow
19—Lt. Broomfield	Lt. Cutter	Pvt. Croft	Pvt. Tully

PERSONNEL OF 90th SQUADRON DURING ARGONNE-MEUSE OFFENSIVE

Commanding Officer — Lieut. Schauffler (until October 22), Lieut. Pierson

Adjutant — Lieut. Lockwood (until October 22), Lieut. Hayden

Operations Officer — Lieut. Adams (until October 17), Lieut. Tillman (until October 22), Lieut. Lowe

"A" FLIGHT

Sgt. 1st Cl. York, in charge of hangar

Pilot	Observer	Crew Chief	Assistant
1—Lt. White (Flight Commander)	Capt. Foster	Chf. Hunsacker	Pvt. Antosh
2—Lt. Livingston	Lt. Shuss	Chf. Auten	Pvt. 1st Cl. Tully
3—Lt. Cowle	Lt. Francis	Chf. De Baun	Pvt. 1st Cl. McWhirter
4—Lt. Conover	Lt. Burger	Chf. O'Connel	Pvt. Blackledge
5—Lt. Hart	Lt. Grier	Chf. Tiller	Pvt. 1st Cl. Stone
6—Lt. Whitehead		Sgt. 1st. Cl. Chew	Pvt. 1st Cl. Pino

"B" FLIGHT

Sgt. 1st Cl. Blake, in charge of hangar

Pilot	Observer	Crew Chief	Assistant
7—Lt. Greist (Flight Commander)	Lt. Tillman	Sgt. Goodman	Pvt. 1st Cl. King
8—Lt. Neidecker	Lt. Lake	Sgt. Medlin	Pvt. 1st Cl. Buckley
9—Lt. Ellis	Lt. Borden	Cpl. Barton	Pvt. Race
10—Lt. Kinsley	Lt. Lowe	Sgt. Cargill	Pvt. 1stCl. Killman
11—Lt. Bovard	Lt. Foster	Sgt. Clifton	Pvt. 1st Cl. Kendricks
12—Lt. Carver	Lt. Lindstrom	Chf. Farrand	Cpl. Bunning

"C" FLIGHT

Sgt. 1st Cl. Johnson, in charge of hangar

Pilot	Observer	Crew Chief	Assistant
14—Lt. Pierson (Flight Commander until October 22)	Lt. Hayden	Chf. 1st Cl. Richey	Chf. 1st Cl. Carson
15—Lt. Lee	Lt. Walden	Sgt. Jaeger	Pvt. 1st Cl. Larson
16—Lt. Rohrer	Lt. Vinson	Chf. Pheiffer	Pvt. 1st Cl. Lackey
17—Lt. Pike	Lt. Parr	Sgt. 1st Cl. Ford	Pvt. De Young
18—Lt. Dorrance		Chf. Craig	Sgt. Brown
19—Lt. Young (Flight Commander, Oct. 22-Nov. 11)	Lt. Bogle	Sgt. Bair	Cpl. Morrow
20—Lt. Broomfield	Lt. Cutter	Cpl. Croft	Pvt. 1st Cl. Clickner

ROSTER

OFFICERS

Adams, Morton B. . . . 1st Lieut. F. A., Observer
817 Stahlman Bldg., Nashville, Tenn.

Baker, Warren L. . . . . . 2nd Lieut., Observer
409 W. Sixth St., Lexington, Ky.

Black, Asa R. . . . . . 1st Lieut. A. S., Observer

Blekre, Ferdinand . . . . . 1st Lieut. Cav., Observer
Lanesboro, Minn.

Bogle, Henry C. . . . . 2nd Lieut. F. A., Observer
843 E. Jefferson Ave., Detroit, Mich.

Borden, Horace L. . . . . . 2nd Lieut. S. C., Observer
Suite 26, 204 Hemenway St., Boston, Mass.

Bovard, James M. . . . . 1st Lieut. A. S., Pilot
682 Avenue C, Bayonne, N. J.

Burger, Valentine J. . . . . 2nd Lieut. Inf., Observer
135 Christie St., Leonia, N. J.

Carver, Leland M. . . . . . 1st Lieut. A. S., Pilot
American Flying Club, 11 E. 38th St., New York City

Conover, Harvey . . . . . 1st Lieut. A. S., Pilot
Hinsdale, Ill.

Crook, Wilson W. . . . . 2nd Lieut. A. S., Pilot
919 Annex Ave., Dallas, Texas

Derby, Richard . . . . 1st Lieut. C. A. C., Observer

Dorrance, George W. . . . 2nd Lieut. A. S., Observer
9 Courtlandt Place, Houston, Texas

Elliott, William, Jr. . . . . 1st Lieut. Cav., Observer
522 West End Ave., New York City

Ellis, Henry R. . . . . . 1st Lieut. A. S., Pilot
Oxford Road, New Hartford, N. Y.

Foster A. T. . . . . . 1st Lieut. F. A., Observer
Derby Line, Vt.

Foster, Harry . . . . . . Capt. Cav., Observer
113 W. 84th St., New York City

Francis, Walter L.   .   .   .   .   2nd Lieut. Inf., Observer
             Glastonbury, Conn.

Freeman, Harry B.   .   .   .   .   1st Lieut. A. S., Pilot
          Lynnfield Center, Mass.

Gallop, Harold M.   .   .   .   .   Capt. A. S., Pilot
           Langley Field, Va.

Greist, E. Harold   .   .   .   .   1st Lieut. A. S., Pilot
         61 N. Clay St., Hinsdale, Ill.

Grier, Alexander T.   .   .   .   2nd Lieut. Inf., Observer
        703 N. Division St., Salisbury, Md.

Hackett, William H. Y.   .   .   .   1st Lieut. A. S., Adjt.
        242 Canton Ave., Milton, Mass.

Hall, Levi M.   .   .   .   .   2nd Lieut. A. S., Pilot
       308 Gramercy Ave., Minneapolis, Minn.

Hart, Floyd H. .   .   .   .   .   2nd Lieut. A. S., Pilot
         Edgevale Orchard, Medford, Ore.

Harrison, Randolph C.   .   .   .   2nd Lieut. F. A., Observer
        Monroe Terrace, Richmond, Va.

Hayden, Van B. .   .   .   .   2nd Lieut. A. S., Observer
        729 Franklin St., Keokuk, Iowa

Hendricks, T. N.   .   .   .   2nd Lieut. F. A., Observer
            Nashville, Ga.

Hume, Allen P.   .   .   .   .   .   .   Capt. A. S.
           Washington, D. C.

Kinsley, Wilburt E.   .   .   .   2nd Lieut. A. S., Pilot
        99 Cambridge St., Winchester, Mass.

Kirschner, Frederick   .   .   .   2nd Lieut. Ord.
        906 Lakeside Place, Chicago, Ill.

Lacy, Clive W.   .   .   .   2nd Lieut. Ord., Armament
       16 Harvard Terrace, Boston, Mass.

Lake, Horace A.   .   .   .   2nd Lieut. Inf., Observer
       3528 T St., N. W., Washington, D. C.

Lee, Marshall G.   .   .   .   1st Lieut. A. S., Pilot
       1255 Oak Knoll Ave., Pasadena, Calif.

Lindstrom, Gustaf T.   .   .   2nd Lieut. S. C., Observer
        2025 Sixth Ave., Moline, Ill.

Livingston, John W.   .   .   .   1st Lieut. A. S., Pilot
       1623 Eighth Ave., Moline, Ill.

Livingston, J. J.   .   .   .   1st Lieut. M. C., Surgeon
220 W. Ferguson St., Tyler, Texas

Lockwood, Alan E.   .   .   1st Lieut. A. S., Engineer and Adjt.
135 East Ave., Norwalk, Conn.

Looney, Ralph D.   .   .   1st Lieut. A. S., Supply Officer
Calvert, Texas

Lowe, William G.   .   .   .   Captain U. S. M. C., Observer
Fountain City, Knoxville, Tenn.

McSherry, F. D.   .   .   .   .
Gordon Bldg., McAlester, Okla.

Neidecker, Bertrand C.   .   .   .   1st Lieut. A. S., Pilot
Guaranty Trust Co., 140 Broadway, New York City

O'Connor, Arthur J.   .   .   .   2nd Lieut. A. S., Radio Officer
127 20th St., Milwaukee, Wis.

Parr, Arthur E.   .   .   .   2nd Lieut. A. S., Observer
706 E. Bell St., Bloomington, Ill.

Pike, Glenn M.   .   .   .   .   1st Lieut. A. S., Pilot
American Flying Club, 11 E. 38th St., New York City

Phillips, Hubert N.   .   .   .   1st Lieut. F. A., Observer
1705 Hague Ave., St. Paul, Minn.

Pierson, Norris E.   .   .   .   Captain A. S., Pilot
61 Broad St., Stamford, Conn.

Phinzy, Jack   .   .   .   .   .   1st Lieut., A. S.

Rohrer, Loren E.   .   .   .   .   1st Lieut., A. S., Pilot
5834 Center Ave., Pittsburgh, Pa.

Schauffler, William G., Jr.   .   .   .   Major A. S., Pilot
Care of Air Service, U. S. Army

Sherrick, John C.   .   .   .   1st Lieut. A. S., Observer
317 E. Broadway, Monmouth, Ill.

Shuss, Pressley B.   .   .   .   1st Lieut. A. S., Observer
Stearns Light & Power Co., Ludington, Mich.

Simpson, Leslie B.   .   .   .   .   1st Lieut. A. S., Pilot
1338 Kellam Ave., Los Angeles, Calif.

Sullivan, Arthur M.   .   .   .   2nd Lieut. F. A., Observer
Minneapolis, Minn.

Tillman, Fred A.   .   .   .   2nd Lieut. F. A., Observer
Congressional Offices, Washington, D. C.

"C" FLIGHT CREWS   SNAPPED AROUND THE HANGAR   THE BATHHOUSE

BEEZER–THE WILD BOAR   THE PENNANT CHASERS

HOME SWEET HOME   CLEMENCAU PAYS A VISIT

Vinson, Fred L. . . . . 2nd Lieut. F. A., Observer
        1459 N St., N. W., Washingthon, D. C.

Walden, Donald M. . . . 2nd Lieut. F. A., Observer
        294 Jefferson Ave., Brooklyn, N. Y.

Wallace, John H. . . . . 2nd Lieut. A. S., Engineer
        Rockwall, Texas

White, Merritt O. . . . . . 1st Lieut. A. S., Pilot
        Tyngsboro, Mass.

Whitehead, George W. . . . . 2nd Lieut. A. S., Pilot
        46 Ashland Ave., Buffalo, N. Y.

Young, John S. . . . . . 1st Lieut. A. S., Pilot
        National Life Ins. Bldg., Montpelier, Vt.

ENLISTED MEN

Adler, Philip, Pvt. . . . . Left before active service
        Omaha, Nebr.

Alhofen, Harry J., Pvt. . . . . . . Orderly
        c/o Deisel, 108 Fulton Ave., Greenville, N. J.

Allman, Orrie . . . . . Left before active service
        New York City

Anchors, Roy R. . . . . Plane Crews
        718 Seventh St., New Kensington, Pa.

Antosh, Charles, Pvt. 1st Cl. . . . . Plane Crews
        464 28th St., Detroit, Mich.

Armstrong, Frederick A., Pvt. 1st Cl. . . . Blacksmith
        201 So. Main St., Kirksville, Mo.

Auten, Frank B., Chfr. . . . . . . Crew Chief
        Highland, Ill.

Baer, Bankard F., Sgt. 1st Cl. . . . Armament, C Flight
        Raspeburg, Md.

Bair, Roy F., Sgt. . . . . Crew Chief
        The Dalles, Ore.

Barton, Clyde J., Cpl. . . . . . . Crew Chief
        Greenfield, Tenn.

Bertonz, George C., Pvt. 1st Cl. . . . . Plane Crews
        2059 W. 23rd St., Chicago, Ill.

Billings, Thomas M., Chfr. . . Transportation, Chauffeur
        111 N. Summit St., Arkansas City, Kans.

Bittle, Roy L., Sgt. 1st Cl. . . . . . . Radio, B Flight
724 S. Liberty St., Independence, Mo.

Blackledge, LeRoy J., Cpl. . . . . . Plane Crews
1232 Philo St., Scranton, Pa.

Blake, Councell A., Sgt. 1st Cl. . In Charge of Crews, B Flight
Easton, Md.

Blake, Karl G., Pvt. . . . . . . Squadron Office
Vinton, Ohio

Bly, Chris M., Pvt. . . . . . Wireless Operator
Mount Pocono, Pa.

Bodvin, William L., Cpl. . . . . . . Armament
1068 E. 27th St., N., Portland, Ore.

Boersma, Barney, Pvt. . . . . Left before active service
667 N. Leonard St., Grand Rapids, Mich.

Boyle, William, Sgt. . . . . Transportation Mechanic
Box 818, Billings, Mont.

Bradley, Harold C., Pvt. 1st Cl. . . . . . Orderly
563 Winewood Ave., Detroit, Mich.

Brannan, William E., Pvt. . . . .
2614 Market St., St. Louis, Mo.

Brandt, Arthur P., Chfr. . . . Transportation, Chauffeur
309 Alger St., Saginaw, Mich.

Braun, Charles H., Pvt. . . . . . . Plane Crews
Houston, Me.

Brickey, Wilfred, Pvt. 1st Cl. . . . . . Plane Crews
Middlebury, Vt.

Brochu, Albert J., Pvt. . . . . Orderly
Plainfield, Conn.

Brooks, Lewis R. . . . . . . Squadron Office
Kutztown, Pa.

Broome, George S., Chfr. . . . Transportation, Chauffeur
2956 Wabash Ave., Chicago, Ill.

Brown, George, Pvt. . . . . Orderly
Carmi, Ill.

Brown, Porter J., Sgt. . . . . . . Crew Chief
Seymore, Texas

Brown, William L., Pvt. . . . Left before active service
McKinney, Texas

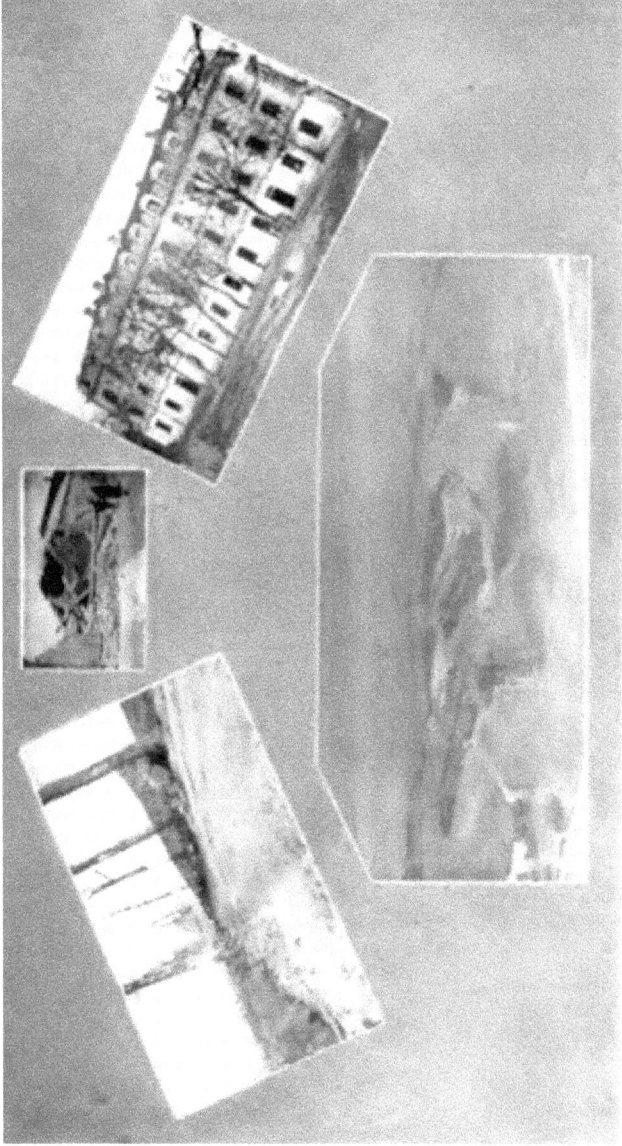

NEAR THE LINE   COLOMBES–AFTER THE RAID   AT LABOURNE

A DEFENDER OF VERDUN

Brudnicki, Czeslaw, Pvt. . . . . Squadron, Shoe Maker
2441 Walton St., Chicago, Ill.

Brunk, Charles E., Pvt. . . . . Left before active service
Pomeroy, Wash.

Buckley, Edward L., Pvt. 1st Cl. . . . . Plane Crews
56 Main St., Dobbs Ferry, N. Y.

Bunn, Carl H., Pvt. . . . . Transportation, Chauffeur
2417 Commerce St., Dallas, Texas

Bunning, Adolph J., Pvt., 1st Cl. . . . . Plane Crews
367 E. Tenth St., Portland, Ore.

Busch, William V., Sgt. . . . Left before active service
1082 Harrison Ave., Beloit, Wis.

Busser, John R., Pvt. . . . . Left before active service
632 S. Champion Ave., Columbus, Ohio

Butler, Joseph F., Sgt. . . . . . . E. & R. Shops
495 N. Commercial St., Salem, Ore.

Buttrill, Raiford R. . . . . Left before active service
Dublin, Texas

Byrth, Thomas M., Sgt. 1st Cl. . . . . Squadron Office
629 Rockdale Ave., Avondale, Cincinnati, Ohio

Cargill, William H., Chfr. . . . . Crew Chief
Jonesville, Texas

Carson, Willard F., Sgt. 1st Cl. . . . . Crew Chief
Toledo, Ore.

Chancellor, Abe., Pvt. . . . Transportation, Motorcycle
Box 92, Snyder, Okla.

Chew, George A., Sgt. 1st Cl. . . . . Crew Chief
Santa Clara, Calif.

Chittenden, Edwin A., Chfr. . . Transportation, Chauffeur
619 Magnolia Ave., Sandford, Fla.

Clark, Howard L., Pvt. . . . Transportation, Chauffeur
P. O. Box 159, Bellevue, Idaho

Clickner, Walter G., Chfr. . . . . . Plane Crews
254 Schermerhorn St., Brooklyn, N. Y.

Clifton, Joseph E., Sgt. . . . . . Crew Chief
838 Sherman St., Johnstown, Pa.

Collins, Carter, Pvt. . . . .
Seymour, Conn.

Conn, James H., Pvt. . . . . Transportation, Chauffeur
701 Owen St., Saginaw, Mich.

Conner, John A., Chfr. . . . Transportation, Chauffeur
W. Fourth Ave., Corsicana, Texas

Connors, James A., Pvt. . . . . . . Plane Crews
372 Chestnut St., Kingstown, Pa.

Corcoran, Timothy J., Pvt. . . . . . . Orderly
49 Hedley St., Providence, R. I.

Craig, Roscoe J., Sgt. . . . . . Crew Chief
Indianola, Nebr.

Croft, Lewin R., Pvt. 1st Cl. . . . . . Crew Chief
Box 54, Stephenville, Texas

Cross, George W., Pvt. . . . . Left before active service
Pittsburg, Texas

Cummins, James W., Sgt. 1st Cl. . . . . Machine Shop
1016 W. Sears St., Denison, Tex.

Cummings, Dewey, Pvt. . . . . Orderly
1304 Broadway, Mattoon, Ill.

Curry, Alfred E., Cpl. . . . . . . Field Office
Yuma, Colo.

Davy, Jesse O., Pvt. . . . . . Field Lighting System
Carlson, N. D.

De Baun, Fay F., Sgt. . . . . . . Crew Chief
Linton, Ind.

De Young, Jake R., Pvt. . . . . . . Plane Crews
Rock Valley, Iowa

Dewey, La Vern I., Pvt. . . . Left before active service
506 Allen St., Adrian, Mich.

Dyke, Fred M., Pvt. . . . . Left before active service
Gilmer, Texas

Ebright Victor, Chfr. . . . Transportation, Chauffeur
2314 Victor St., Bellingham, Wash.

Emich, William L., Pvt. 1st Cl. . . . . . Cook
5144 Reisters Town Road, Arlington, Md.

England, Arlett, Cfr. 1st Cl. . . Transportation, Chauffeur
Athens, Texas

England, Michael P., Pvt. . . . Left before active service
Cork, Ireland

Erickson, Harvey E., Cpl. . . . . . Squadron Office
    112 S. Foster St., Merrill, Wisc.

Farmer, William J., Pvt. 1st Cl. . . Transportation, Motorcycle
    321 E. 44th St., So., Portland, Ore.

Farrand, George E., Chfr. . . . . . Crew Chief
    Pittsfield, Ill.

Field, Floyd C. . . . . . Transportation, Chauffeur
    Thomas, N. M.

Fitzgerald, Ben T., Pvt. 1st Cl. . . . . Water Supply
    Kemp, Texas

Fletcher, Ray C., Pvt. . . . . Left before active service
    25 St. Louis St., Burlington, Vt.

Ford, Lyle H., Sgt. . . . . . Crew Chief
    Sioux City, Iowa

Forrest, Harley D., Pvt. . . . Transportation, Chauffeur
    318 W. Park St., Toledo, Ohio

Frost, George F., Chfr. . . . . . Cook
    801 Hosmer St., Lansing, Mich.

Franklin, Lex., Chfr. . . . Transportation, Motorcycle
    Eureka, Ind.

Fridge, Clifford V., Pvt. . . . . . Squadron Office
    Baton Rouge, La.

Frye, Hershel E. . . . . . E. & R.
    65 W. Pleasant St., Noblesville, Ind.

Galvin, Thomas J. . . . .
    510 Seventh St., Bismark, N. D.

Garett, John S., Cpl. . . . . . Radio, C Flight
    Fifth St., Bernis, Tenn.

Garwood, Harry W. . . . . . . Orderly
    345 Garfield Ave., Cypress, N. Y.

Gilley, Herbert O., Pvt. . . . . . Cook
    423 Lane St., Waterloo, Iowa

Giltner, Arthur J., Cook . . . . . Cook
    Conroe, Texas

Goodman, Ollen E., Sgt. 1st Cl. . . . Crew Chief
    1445 College Ave., Clarksville, Texas

Gottselig, Christian . . . .
    802 St. Joseph St., Lancaster, Pa.

Grammer, George G., Cpl. . . . . . . Supply Dept.
Pittsburg, Texas

Grant, Ulysses L., Pvt. . . . . Cook
Manteno, Ill.

Greer, Edwin R., M. S. E. . . . Squadron Sergeant Major
Pittsburg, Texas

Gregory, Armen, Pvt. . . . . Orderly
79½ Kendall Ave., Detroit, Mich.

Grice, Olley R., Chfr. . . . . . . Crew Chief
Brookhaven, Miss.

Griffin, Clinton J., Sgt. . . . . E. & R.
Portland, Ore.

Griffith, James A., Sgt. 1st Cl. . . . . . Armament
Walthill, Nebr.

Grisso, Henry N., Pvt. . . . .
327 W. Washington St., Springfield, Ohio

Halm, Louis A., Sgt. 1st Cl. . . . . . Machine Shop
418 Harrison St., Piqua, Ohio

Halpin, William J., Pvt. . . . . Bugler
Chatfield, Minn.

Hall, Edward J. . . . . . . Armament, A Flight
R. R. No. 5, Battle Creek, Mich.

Hancock, Hiram R., Cpl. . . . . . Mail Orderly
Maysville, Ga.

Hankins, Walter H., Sgt. 1st Cl. . . . Chief of E. & R.
Castle Rock, Wash.

Hardesty, Hiram H., Pvt. . . . Transportation, Motorcycle
R. R. No. 3, Piqua, Ohio

Harnish, Frank D., Sgt. . . . . . Squadron Office
O'Neil, Nebr.

Harrison, Harvey R., Pvt. . . . .
West Salem, Ill.

Harsha, Orlando N., Pvt. 1st Cl. . . . . Radio Operator
407 N. Seventh St., Vincennes, Ind.

Harvel, Jess H., Pvt. . . . . Transportation, Mechanic
314 W. Maple St., Oklahoma City, Okla.

Heckle, Charles E., Pvt. . . . .
525 Taylor St., Scranton, Pa.

Hengy, George C., Sgt. . . . Injured and sent to hospital
                              Dallas, Texas

Henry, Aaron W., Cpl. . . . . E. & R.
                              Apollo, Pa.

Herold, Joseph, Pvt. . . . .
                              Slater, Wyo.

Herren, Joseph N., Pvt. . . . . . . Orderly
                              May, Okla.

Heiser, Charles W., Pvt. . . . . . . Cook
                              3125 W. 63rd St., Chicago, Ill.

Higgins, Leon W., Pvt. . . . . . Provost Sergeant
                              19508 Chichester Ave., Hollis, L. I., N. Y.

Hill, Frank T., Chfr. . . . . . . Machine Shop
                              907 N. Carey St., Baltimore, Md.

Hill, Louis H., Sgt. 1st Cl. . . . . . Mess Sergeant
                              2009 Webster St., Oakland, Calif.

Honeycutt, Baker M., Pvt. . . . . . Plane Crews
                              Greenwood, La.

Horn, Paul, Pvt. . . . .
                              Moose Head, Minn.

Houtz, Harry L., Pvt. 1st Cl. . . . . . Orderly
                              213 Schuylkill Ave., Tamaka, Pa.

Hubbell, Aaron W., Sgt. 1st Cl. . . . Chief Radio Operator
                              1520 Lincoln Ave., Walnut Hills, Cincinnati, Ohio

Hughart, Walter, Pvt. . . . .
                              Box 34, Saverton, Mo.

Hunsaker, Omer L., Chfr. . . . . . . Crew Chief
                              Golden, Ill.

Hyde, James R., Pvt. . . . . . . Transportation
                              659 Wellington Ave., Chicago

Irwin, William, Pvt. . . . .
                              Gen. Del., Danville, Ill.

Isaacson, Walter S. . . . . Plane Crews
                              2625 Pillsbury Ave., Minneapolis, Minn.

Jaeger, George H., Sgt. . . . . . Plane Crews
                              Iroquois Falls, New Ontario, Canada

Jones, Robert O., Sgt. 1st Cl. . . . . Supply Sergeant
                              Maybank, Texas

Johnson, Paul J., Sgt. 1st Cl. . . In charge of crews, C Flight
    118 S. Fourth St., Union City, Tenn.

Justus, Edward C., Chfr. . . . Transportation, Chauffeur
    1107 W. Main St., Urbana, Ill.

Kaake, William R., Pvt. . . . . Cook
    466 Woodlawn Ave., Detroit, Mich.

Ketterman, Harry A., Pvt. . . . Left before active service
    30 N. 17th St., Portland, Ore.

Key, Ellis W., M. S. E. . . . . Transportation Chief
    Bryan, Ohio

Killman, William H., Pvt. 1st Cl. . . . . Plane Crews
    15 S. Elwood Ave., Baltimore, Md.

Kimball, Heber C., Pvt. . . . .
    Safford, Ariz.

Kendricks, William G., Pvt. 1st Cl. . . . Plane Crews
    99 N. Electric Ave., Alhambra, Calif.

King, Hugh R., Pvt. 1st Cl. . . . . . Plane Crews
    112 S. Prospect St., Connelsville, Pa.

King, Wade C., Sgt. 1st Cl. . . . . Armament Chief
    Mill St., Louisville, Ohio

Klapsch, Fred., Pvt. . . . . Left before active service
    399 Howard St., Detroit, Mich.

Klippstein, Theodore A., Cpl. . . . . Squadron Office
    Morris, Minn.

Lackey, Stamie, Pvt. 1st Cl. . . . . . Plane Crews
    Hiddenite, N. C.

Lambert, Lucas A., M. S. E. . . . . . Machine Shop
    North Windsor, Md.

La Mont, George A. . . . . Orderly
    5728 Julian St., St. Louis, Mo.

Lane, Clifford H., Cook . . . . Cook
    2001 E. Sixth St., Pueblo, Colo.

Larson, Elmer P., Pvt. . . . . . . Plane Crews
    712 Barnes St., Lewistown, Mont.

Layton, Anthony A., Pvt. 1st Cl. . . . . Orderly
    2209 N. Ninth St., St. Louis, Mo.

Lekven, Carl, Pvt. 1st Cl. . . . . . . Orderly
    110 Passaic Ave., Harrison, N. J.

Lewis, Rufus, Pvt. . . . .
Springfield, Minn.

Love, John E., Pvt. . . . .
Tompkinsville, Md.

Loveridge, William G., Sgt. . . . . Armament, B Flight
723 E. Arcadia Ave., Peoria, Ill.

Martin, Fred L., Cpl. . . . . E. & R.
Mossyrock, Wash.

McAndrews, Robert S., Pvt. . . Transportation, Motorcycle
Lane, Idaho

McCann, Patrick J., Pvt. 1st Cl. . . . .
189 Whittenton St., Taunton, Mass.

McDowell, Ralph L., Cook . . . . Cook
647 S. 14th St., Salem, Ore.

McLay, Charles R., Pvt. . . . . Cook
Portland, Ore.

McReynolds, Thomas R., Pvt. . . Left before active service
706 Wabash Ave., Ottumwa, Iowa

McVicar, Clarence V., Pvt. . . . .
Wetumpka, Ala.

McWhirter, Richard C., Pvt. 1st Cl. . . . . . Plane Crews
306 McBrayer St., Shelby, N. C.

Mason, Thomas M., Cpl. . . . . . . Supply Dept.
c/o The Murray Co., Atlanta, Ga.

Mathieu, Frank, Pvt. . . . . . . Squadron Tailor
7 Chestnut St., Spencer, Mass.

Medlin, George B., Sgt. 1st Cl. . . . . . Crew Chief
Galatia, Ill.

Meullier, Ray W., Cfr. 1st Cl. . . Motorcycle Dispatch Rider
c/o Dr. Meullier, Vergennes, Vt.

Miller, Arthur P., Sgt. . . . . . Left for pilot school
Nelighy, Nebr.

Mills, Joe, Pvt. . . . . . . Left before active service
Pawhuska, Okla.

Monahan, James H., Pvt. . . . .
4 Cottage St., Marblehead, Mass.

Morrow, Hoy, Cpl. . . . . Plane Crews
Parkville, Mo.

Mulcahy, Charles R., Pvt. . . . . . . Armament
98 Cleveland Ave., North Adams, Mass.

Neuendorf, Pearleao, Pvt. . . . .
Essex, Ontario, Canada

Nerisen, Baldie, Pvt. . . . . Carpenter
412 N. Fourth St., Albuquerque, N. M.

Nolting, Ray E., Pvt. . . . . Orderly
4719 Hammett Pl., St. Louis, Mo.

O'Connell, Dan P., Sgt. 1st Cl. . . . . . Crew Chief
22 N. 20th St., Portland, Ore.

Oehlert, Herschel E., Pvt. . . . Left before active service
Woodburn, Iowa

Pfeiffer, Herbert H., Sgt. 1st Cl. . . . . Crew Chief
Hooper, Nebt.

Pino, August J., Pvt. 1st Cl. . . . . . Plane Crews
615 Baronne St., New Orleans, La.

Quandt, Ray J., Pvt. . . . . Transportation Chauffeur
Royalton, Wisc.

Quinn, Harry J., Pvt. . . . . Came home with Squadron
2601 W. Third St., Chester, Pa.

Race, Harold L., Pvt. . . . . . . Plane Crews
106 South Ave., Marshaltown, Iowa

Raikes, Lawrence W., Pvt. . . . . . Squadron Barber
R. F. D. "B," Box 216, Bentonville, Kans.

Rich, David A., M. S. E. . . . . . Machine Shop
Heard National Bank, Jacksonville, Fla.

Richardson, Delmer E., Sgt. . . . . . Armament
Lawrence, Mass.

Richey, Owen, Chfr. 1st Cl. . . . . . Crew Chief
Olmsted, Ill.

Sanquist, Evald, Sgt. . . . . . . E. & R. Shops
Natick Ave., Greenwood, R. I.

Savage, Arthur F., Pvt. . . . . Orderly
R. F. D., Box 44, Montague, Mass.

Scudder, George D., Pvt. . . . . . . Orderly
83 Broad St., Bethlehem, Pa.

Sharp, William M., Cpl. . . . . . . Field Office
Philomath, Ore.

"You're next"
FIELD AT BETHLAINVILLEE

"C" FLIGHT CREWS
OFF FOR ANOTHER SECTOR

IT WAS A HARD LIFE (?)
"OPEN FOR BUSINESS"

Sill, Roscoe T., Sgt. 1st Cl. . . . . . . Transportation
915 E. 16th St., University Place, Nebr.

Sload, Charles L., Pvt. . . . .
1224 Market St., Harrisburg, Pa.

Small, Fred W., M. S. E. . . . . . . Machine Shop
Box 891, Nowata, Okla.

Stacy, Noel C., Pvt. . . . . Plane Crews
405 Pendleton Ave., St. Joseph, Mo.

Stetson, Henry A., Chfr. 1st Cl. . . . . Transportation
Pueblo, Colo.

Stewart, Harold E., Pvt. . . . . Cook
Golden, Ill.

St. John, Howard K. . . . . . Left before active service
1215 W. 40th St., Oklahoma City, Okla.

Stierwalt, John E., Cook . . . . Cook
Murray, Iowa

Stone, George T., Pvt. . . . . . . Plane Crews
2728 W. 36th Ave., Denver, Colo.

Strugatz, Geo. H., Pvt. . . . . Orderly
Springfield Ave., Queens, N. Y.

Swank, John F., Cook . . . . Cook
2509 Everett St., Houston, Texas

Sytek, Henry F., Cpl. . . . . Supply Dept.
737 Sixth St., Grand Rapids, Mich.

Swearengen, Clarence A., Pvt. . . . .
401 Poplar St., West Terre Haute, Ind.

Taylor, Harold, Pvt. . . . . . Transportation, Motorcycle
Carson Lake, Minn.

Tiller, Louin, Sgt. . . . . Crew Chief
R. F. D. No. 1, Jones, Okla.

Tipps, Charles R. . . . . Transportation
Canadian, Texas

Tooher, James C. . . . . Orderly
56 Sound Ave., Stamford, Conn.

Toye, Henry H., Cook . . . . Cook
Broken Arrow, Okla.

Tully, John L., Pvt. 1st Cl. . . . . . . Plane Crews
Dorset, Vt.

97

Van Sickle, Arthur W., Sgt. . . . . . . Crew Chief
        c/o Maj. Schauffler, Kelly Field, Texas

Wade, W. Denson, Cpl. . . . . . . Supply Dept.
        Cochran, Ga.

Walsh, Joseph S., Cpl. . . . .
        Freemansburg, W. Va.

White, Ira H., Pvt. . . . . Orderly
        Robinson, Kans.

Wilson, Herman R. . . . .
        3611 Howell St., Dallas, Texas

York, Edwin B., Sgt. 1st Cl. . . In Charge of Crews, A Flight
        Port Republic, N. J.

Zelesnig, Frank, Cook . . . . Cook
        San Francisco, Calif.

MEDICAL DETACHMENT

Baird, Sanford R. . . . . . . Fort Worth Texas

Daniel, Doog, Pvt. . . . . Butler, Texas

Davis, Arthur J., Pvt. . . . . . . Florence, Texas

Dolive, Charles W., Sgt. . . . P. O. Box 12, Oakhurst, Texas

Kempf, Charles W., Pvt. . . 760 Atlantic Ave., Lancaster, Pa.

Lindgren, Pete, Pvt. . . Rt. No. 3, Box 31, Vancouver, Wash.

Love, Hugh C., Pvt. . . 320 E. Third Ave., Gastonia, N. C.

BREGUET

CASUALTIES

Baldwin, ——— . . . . . 2nd Lieut., A. S.
380-B Kane Place, Milwaukee, Wisc.
Killed in railroad wreck, December, 1918

Broomfield, Hugh . . . . . 1st Lieut. A. S., Pilot
527 Tacoma Ave., Portland, Ore.
Killed in action, October 21, 1918

Bolt, ——— . . . . . . 1st Lieut. F. A., Observer
New York City
Killed in action at Chateau Thierry, with 1st Aero Squadron

Cook, Harry . . . . 2nd Lieut. A. S.
Killed in railroad wreck, December, 1918

Cutter, Edward B. . . . . 1st Lieut. F. A., Observer
Anoka, Minn.
Killed in action, October 21, 1918

Cowle, Harland H. . . . . . . 1st Lieut. A. S., Pilot
164 Poplar St., Conneaut, Ohio
Died of pneumonia in base hospital, December, 1918

Hathaway, Edward T. . . . . 1st Lieut. A. S., Pilot
Killed in accident, June, 1918

Maynor, Elbridge W. . . . . 2nd Lieut. A. S., Observer
Killed in accident, June, 1918

Merz, Harold B. . . . . . . 1st Lieut. A. S., Pilot
Killed in accident, December, 1918

Patterson, A. B. . . . . . . 1st Lieut. A. S., Pilot
438 Franklin Ave., Wilkinsburg, Pa.
Killed in action, October 29, 1918, with 93rd Aero Squadron

ENLISTED MEN

Engdahl, Carl A. . . . 42 Mt. Elliott Ave., Detroit, Mich.
Died of pneumonia, January 27, 1918

Gipson, Antony W. . . . . Lawton, Okla.
Killed in accident, April 29, 1918

History of the 91st Aero Squadron
Air Service U. S. A.

AMANTY, MAY 20TH, 1918

Left to right, standing:

Lt. Herbert A. Schaffner, promoted to Capt., commanding 85th Aero Squadron; Ralph W. Stone, Engineering Officer; Thomas M. Jervey, Ordnance Officer, D. S. C.; Kingman Douglass, D. S. C., promoted to Capt.; Horace M. Guilbert, Croix de Guerre; F. Vernon Foster, prisoner, wounded; Howard G. Mayes, prisoner, wounded; Paul H. Hughey, killed in action; Denver F. Graw, medical officer, promoted to Capt.; Alfred W. Lawson, prisoner; Samuel K. Downing, Supply Officer; John W. Van Heuvel, Croix de Guerre, wounded; Blanchard B. Battle, prisoner.

Sitting:

George C. Kenney, D. S. C.; Massey Hill, D. S. C., promoted to Capt., commanding 24th Aero Squadron; Everett R. Cook, D. S. C., promoted to Capt., commanding 91st Aero Squadron; Hugh L. Fontaine, D. S. C., transferred to 47th Aero Squadron; Willis A. Diekema, D. S. C., promoted to Capt., commanding 9th Aero Squadron; Victor H. Strahm, D. S. C., promoted to Capt.; Major John N. Reynolds, D. S. C. with oak leaf, promoted to Lt. Col., commanding 1st Army Observation Group; Alan P. Hume, Adjutant; Clearton H. Reynolds, D. S. C., promoted to Capt., commanding 104th Aero Squadron; John H. Lambert, D. S. C.; Asher E. Kelty, D. S. C., killed in action.

Contents

DEDICATED TO
"MAJOR JOHN"

MAJOR JOHN REYNOLDS

History of the 91st Aero Squadron

Born—On August 20, 1917, at Kelly Field, San Antonio, Texas, to Uncle Sam and Columbia, an Aero Squadron, their 91st.

The 91st Aero Squadron, Aviation Section, Signal Corps, U, S. A., to give the babe its full name, was ushered into the world on the hottest of hot Kelly Field days. For a while it looked as though the hardiest of constitutions would succumb, but true to the form it was destined to exhibit later on, the hotter things got, the better the new-born squadron thrived.

On this day the squadron was first officially designated as the 91st, and detachments from Fort Sill, Oklahoma; Fort Leavenworth, Kansas; Jefferson Barracks, Missouri; and Fort Sam Houston, Texas, arrived at frequent intervals and were assigned to the squadron. First Lieutenant Alan P. Hume, A. S,, S. O. R. C, arrived on Sept. 22, and took up his duties as adjutant, the medico, 1st Lieutenant Denver F. Gray, M. O. R. C, arriving a few days later.

Leaving San Anton' on Sept. 30 for Garden City, Long Island, N. Y., the squadron arrived there on Oct. 5, after a journey remembered mainly for. its dust and discomfort, and took possession of Barracks No. 6 at the Aviation Camp. Drill and guard duty kept their minds off other troubles until Oct. 19, when Martin "Chick" Broderick arrived from Kelly Field after a week of "K. P.-ing" with the 100th, to deliver his now famous lecture on "How to Interview a Colonel Without the Sergeant-Major's Permission". The first review of the squadron was held Oct. 25, after a slight delay occasioned by the post adjutant's inability to decide exactly where he should stand during the proceedings. Five o'clock of the morning of Oct. 27 saw the squadron, this time half-frozen, entraining for Pier 60, North River, and that noon the good ship *Adriatic*, R. M. S., pulled out of New York harbour with the now fairly seasoned outfit.

At Halifax, the convoy of seven other ships was picked up, and a quiet, uneventful trip ended on Nov. 10, when Liverpool, with her curious floating docks and her smoky skies, greeted the travellers. The stay here was short, however, and at 3.15 p. m. the squadron pulled out, arriving at Southampton at midnight. The following day H. M. S. *Huntscraft*, No. E216, which in spite of its name proved to be a cattle-ship, started with the 91st for Havre, arriving after numerous delays at 8 a.m. of the Thirteenth. Everyone was allowed to "rest" at the rest-camp there until the next morning at three-thirty, when the squadron left to take the "*Hommes 40, Chevaux 8*" express for their destination, A. E. F. Headquarters at Chaumont, where they arrived at 9 30 p.m. of the 15th, half of the outfit bunking for the night at headquarters, and the rest in the barracks at Hill 402.

The next day, work on the barracks and hangars started and the squadron settled down to this routine, varied by an occasional landing on the field of a French machine, or a squadron "hike" to some nearby town and back. The hoodoo number for the second time figured on the squadron records, when on the morning of Dec. 13 orders came for an immediate move to Amanty. Arriving there the following day, the squadron came under the command of Major J. T. McNary, of the 1st Corps Observation Group. Their first pilot, 1st Lt. Clearton H. Reynolds, was assigned to them at the same time.

Routine work again claimed the attention of the outfit, a Christmas celebration being the only thing to break the monotony. In one of the hangars a huge tree was hung with presents for the children of the town of Amanty, and while the youngsters, lost in admiration of the display, were wondering what else the gods could have in store for them, Lt. Barnaby of the 1st Aero Squadron, flying a "fighting A. R.", landed in front of the hangar. His stepping out of the machine wearing a regulation Santa Claus disguise dumbfounded them for a few moments, and the wonderful Americans had won a place in the hearts of the child population of one French town forever.

Thirteen again got the call when Major Ralph Royce, commanding the 1st Corps Observation Group, appointed Lt. Reynolds on Jan. 13 to take command of the squadron, filling the place of Major McNary, who had been detached three days previously. First Lieutenant Samuel K. Downing was assigned to the squadron as supply officer on the 19th.

The second pilot, 1st Lt. George "Hump" Bryan, reported on Feb. 5.

This month the outfit missed the thirteenth by a narrow margin when Corporal Mobley broke his arm cranking an A. R., on the 12th, the first accident of any kind to be recorded in the squadron files. First Lieutenant Ralph W, Stone, A, S., O, R. C, was assigned as engineering officer on the 16th.

The 22nd of February, however, saw the culmination of the long work of organisation. On that day Major John N. Reynolds, J. M. A., U. S. A., took command, and seventeen pilots, newly arrived from Issoudun (bearing orders dated Feb, 13, to keep up the squadron tradition), were assigned to the 91st, completing the quota of pilots. A more disgruntled crowd of officers can hardly be imagined, as they had all been taken from the chasse training at Issoudun, the hoped-for goal of every flyer, and sent to join what they expected to be an observation squadron flying A. R.'s. But the personality of Major Reynolds worked wonders, and it was only a matter of a few days before the crowd had become welded together into a close association of real friends with a common purpose. This at first was mostly to do anything even hinted at by "Major John", as he became known immediately after the first officers meeting. The roster of pilots who were destined to start the work that afterwards gave the squadron the name of being "the best Army Squadron on the front", to quote Major-General Foulois and Brigadier-General Mitchell, Was now as follows:

Major John N. Reynolds, 1st Lieutenants Blanchard B. Battle, George H. Bryan, Everett R. Cook, Willis A. Diekema, Kingman Douglass, Hugh L. Fontaine, F. Vernon Foster, Horace M. Guilbert, Maury Hill, Paul H. Hughey, Asher E. Kelty, George C. Kenney, John H. Lambert, Alfred W. Lawson, Howard G, Mayes, Clearton H. Reynolds, Herbert A. Schaffner, Victor H. Strahm, and John W. Van Heuvel,

The squadron now settled down to three months of forced inactivity, disturbed occasionally by rumours that they were to go over the lines in A. R.'s, until it began to look as though the 91st was doomed forever to continue its work of taking up observers of the 1st Observation Group for instruction. About the only events to break the monotony were the arrival of 1st Lt. Thomas M. Jervey, O. R. C, as armament officer, and Kenney's crashing in the woods when the motor died after taking off, which got him a broken ankle with two months in the hospital, and the sobriquet of "Bust-'em-Up George" for the rest of the war.

On March 10, Cook, Foster, Lawson, and Van Heuvel were sent off to the aerial gunnery school at Cazaux for a week's training, the intention being for four other members of the squadron to replace them each week until all had received the much-needed course. On arriving at Cazaux, however, their course was held up and they received on training in gunnery at all, and were finally sent back to the squadron after a month's idleness. About the only work of value that they accomplished was the ferrying back from Orlay of some of the A. R.'s to be used for instruction purposes at the 1st Observation Group.

On the way back heavy clouds came up and Cook, who was flying fairly high, lost his way. While he was trying to locate himself the clouds broke up a little, and much to his surprise he saw trenches beneath him, while the air immediately became decorated with a number of little black clouds. It is whispered that the A. R, turned up considerably more than 1600 revolutions on her way back to Amanty from St. Mihiel, where the Archies had distinguished themselves by firing the first shots at a member of the 91st.

The ability of the original pilots of the outfit to converse fluently in French can be directly traced to the frequent gatherings held at Annette's during those dark Amanty days. While Annette and the "Greyhound" alternately sewed on buttons and poured out the stuff that cheers, "the gang", which did not except Major John, would try out its struggling French on the whole family, including the black cat. Even the story of the subsequent change in Annette's occupation can never dispel entirely the charm that the old place has for us. Any of the old crowd would gladly undergo that horrible cross-country trip back to camp, again, for another of the old time gatherings.

Finally the welcome news came that the 91st was to be known as the First American Army Observation Squadron and would fly Salmsons. The first four of these "ships", the last word in French airplane construction, and acknowledged to be the best biplace machine on the front, arrived from Paris on the 21st of April, and others continued to arrive until the 21st of May, when it was considered by headquarters that we had enough to start work with. On the 24th the squadron actually arrived on the front, taking up their quarters on the field near Gondreville-sur-Moselle, Where they were joined by Photo Section No. 2, comprising 24 men under the command of 1st Lt. James S. Suydam, subsequently known as "Photo".

Once again delays were encountered in getting started. The propellers furnished were painted-over affairs that split after a few hours use, and the spark-plugs were of an inferior type that fouled so easily that if was practically impossible to depend on them. If was not until June 3 that the first flight was made over the lines. Major John leading.

In the meantime we had been joined by a number of observers, some of whom had served with the French for a short time previously, Capts. James E. Wallis and Joseph F. Williamson, 1st Lts. Howard T. Baker, Walter Bender, John W. Cousins, Walter R. Lawson, Kenyon Roper, Franz F. Schilling, Howard W. Verwohlt, 2nd Lts. William T. Badham, John C. Henderson, Frederick K. Hirth, Francis B. Lowry, Alonzo M. Seymour, and John H. Snyder coming into the fold as observers, 2nd Lt. Prentice M. Terry reporting as Intelligence Officer, and 2nd Lt.. John E. Wise as Radio Officer. Hume left the squadron on May 30 and Lt. Reynolds acted as adjutant until June 4, when 1st Lt. Roy S. Ripley arrived and took over the position. The flights were also organised, Lt. Reynolds taking the first flight, "Schaff" the second, and Maury Hill the third.

On the 6th, new spark-plugs and twenty-two new "props" were received, and the next morning every ship in commission went over, the majority returning with the news that the Archies were passing good, and exhibiting a number of holes in the ships to prove it. The assignment of observers was completed on the 11th with the arrival of 1st Lt. Leonard C. Hammond. The 12th saw the war really brought home for the first time. Battle and Williamson went over as protection for Mayes and Schilling, who were taking photographs about fifteen kilometres back of the enemy lines. On the way back, going through some clouds. Battle's machine disappeared from view of the photographic ship and did not return to the field.

Inquiries all over the front brought no information, and it was not until June 30 that we learned from a note dropped by a German flyer that they were both prisoners, unwounded. Earlier in the day we also had our first plane brought down by Archie fire. "Diek" and "Bill" Badham went over on a visual mission but evidently their presence was highly undesirable, as from the moment they crossed the lines the anti-aircraft batteries opened up on them, registering some wonderful shots. One of these, coming from a particularly "hot" battery located near Arnaville, punctured the radiator and tore a furrow through "Diek's" helmet. The thermometer rose in jumps when the water started running out, and Diekema headed for home, managing to cross the lines at about a thousand meters altitude, finally landing

"The Archies are hot around Metz today."

safely with about thirty "Archie" holes in his wings and fuselage.

Again the thirteenth was eventful. "Schaff" started on a visual over Metz with "Chief" Bender as observer, leading two other members of the second flight, "Vic" Strahm with "Cap" Wallis, and "Jesus' Lambert with Baker. West of Metz "Vic" became separated from the rest of the formation on the turn, and was almost immediately hopped by three *Pfalz* scouts, who proceeded to put several holes in his ship, luckily doing no material damage. The Boches were kept off by Strahm's manoeuvring and "Cap" Wallis's shooting, and when they reached the lines the enemy headed back for home. In the meantime five other *Pfalzes* had attacked the other two ships, and the chase to the lines was repeated. In this case, however, the two machines could cover each other fairly well, and although they were both badly shot up before they reached the lines the fire of the observers kept the Boches from closing in. Bender shooting one of the enemy machines down out of control. The combat occurred so far back of the lines that confirmation has never been received.

On the 21st the major, aided and abetted by "Back Areas" Terry, instituted a series of examinations on the sector, to make sure that both pilots and observers knew the main features of the ground over which they were to work. First results were extremely gratifying, but the major was not satisfied, and it was owing to this course of careful study that the squadron was able to accomplish much of the valuable work that it did in preparation for the drive at the St. Mihiel salient later on.

An amusing incident occurred on June 25. Cook started out on a visual reconnaissance with "Pop" Seymour on the back seat, and just before crossing the lines, was peaked on by what had hitherto appeared to be a friendly Nieuport. Cook banked over to show his colours, but was greeted with a burst of machine-gun bullets. Slightly annoyed by the occurrence, he *viraged* around and returned the fire, figuring that perhaps the reports were true that the Boches were flying around in some of the recently captured "28's" The intruder withdrew, and Cook continued on his way. When he returned, an investigation trip to the neighbouring pursuit field was made, and there he discovered that a fellow townsman had mistaken him for a Boche biplace machine and had already reported the combat. Apologies were made and each assured the other that a certain girl of Memphis, Tenn., was not the cause of the encounter.

The next few days were ideal for photographic work, and every team that could get off the ground went out on missions covering practically the whole sector. The 1st Pursuit Group had gone to the Chateau-Thierry sector to take part in the commencement of Foch's now famous drive, and all the work of taking pictures was completed without chasse protection. Combats became so common that they were hardly worth mentioning unless some material damage was done or a plane brought down. On June 30 the day's report of forty-two hours, and one hundred and ninety plates exposed, over the lines, so impressed General Giraud of the French VIIIth Army that he sent Major Reynolds a special letter of commendation on his work and the work of the outfit.

While the note that the Germans had dropped telling of the fate of Battle and Williamson was still under discussion, a second plane was entered on the casualty list. A formation of three ships was attacked by nine Boches and during the combat Mayes and Schilling became separated from the rest and did not return. We heard from Mayes some time afterward that during the fight Schilling had been killed and Mayes shot in the head and leg. In spite of his injuries he had brought the machine down safely although he was forced to land some distance behind the enemy lines, where he was taken prisoner and sent to a military hospital.

July fourth seemed about to pass with little more than a mention, but the people of Gondreville refused to allow such sacrilege. Shortly after lunch. While the officers were still around the mess-hall, a procession of children, headed by His Honour the mayor in silk hat and red sash, and a selected delegation of citizens, stopped in front of the shack. After an elaborate speech in token of their appreciation of the work that we were doing for their country, they presented Major Reynolds with a testimonial in the name of the town, and then proceeded to decorate our mess-hall with flowers. The whole officers' personnel of the squadron then fell in with the procession and followed the mayor to the Maison Commune where, after a lunch of French pastry, fruits, and champagne, everyone signed the town book and was given the freedom of the city.

The 12th saw our first replacement. First Lieutenant Edward R. Kenneson reported as pilot, and two days later three new observers, Harry N. Mangan, Harley Perry, and Frederick E. Sieper, all 2nd lieutenants, reported for duty.

On July 16 one of the queer things that make one believe in luck, happened to a two-ship formation that crossed the lines on a daybreak

GONDREVILLE, AUGUST 1ST, 1918

Left to right.

Standing: Stone, Mangan, "Doc" Gray, Baker, Royer, Wallis, Snyder, Nenneson, Sieper, "Al" Lawson, Lambert, Henderson, Guilbert, Lowry, Wise, Badham, Downing, Kenney, and Kelty

Kneeling: Seymour, Hammond, Verwohlt, Chamberlin, Van Hovel, Fontaine, and Perry

Sitting: Hughey, Cook, Diekema, Douglass, Strahm, Hill, Major Reynolds, Ripley, Cousins, Jervey, Sutherland, Schaffner, and Pica.

visual. Guilbert and Seymour and Van Heuvel and Hirth were the two teams. They had just crossed north of Pont-a-Mousson at an altitude of 4800 meters when four Fokkers jumped them, shooting Hirth through the heart and "creasing" Van Heuvel on each side of his head at the first burst. Van was knocked unconscious, and did not come to until he had dropped over 4000 meters, when he found himself on our side of the lines in a steep dive with the motor full on. He managed to pull himself together and landed on his own field, where he protested that he was all right and refused to have his name taken off the flying list even for a day. Guilbert and Seymour in the meantime were having a rather rough time of it. Seymour had his windshield shot off and seven holes in the tourelle around him, while Guilbert had three holes in his Teddy-bear. By alternately going into a spiral and a nose-dive they managed to get away.

In the midst of this shortage of observers, while we were wondering when our regular men would wear out entirely from repeated doubling, Tom Jervey, the ordnance officer, volunteered to go along, "to do a little lookin' and a little shootin'", as he expressed it. He first officially crossed the lines on July 22nd with Schaffner, and this trip started a career of which any observer might well be proud. Flying at various times with practically every one of the older pilots, including Major Reynolds, he is recognised as one of the best observers in the squadron. He has taken visual, protection, and photographic missions, and during this time has engaged in eleven different combats, bringing down three enemy machines for which he has received official credit.

July 27th brought the first promotion, Lt. Reynolds leaving to take command of the newly-formed 104th Observation Squadron, and Diekema taking his place as leader of the first flight. Two additional members of the officers' personnel reported at the same time, 2nd Lt. A. H. Fleck as assistant to Jervey, and 2nd Lt. Clarke S. Sutherland reporting with fifty enlisted men of whom we were badly in need, as our work had become so extensive that if was practically impossible for the enlisted personnel to fake care of things. First Lieutenant Willard J. Chamberlin reported as pilot on the 30th. The day was also marked by the wounding of observer "Shorty" Lawson by anti-aircraft fire while on a visual mission over Vigneulles. He was sent to the hospital, remaining there until the 8th, when he was allowed to come back for light duty until completely recovered.

The squadron lost a good observer and an excellent shot with a

ELECTION OF MESS OFFICERS, GONDREVILLE

pair of Lewis guns when on the first of August orders came through for "Chief" Bender to report to G, H. Q. for headquarters duty.

A week of cloudy and rainy weather, coming at a time when the interest of the squadron was high in their work, finally got on the nerves of some of the crowd, and on the evening of the 10th, Schaff and Baker, and "Jesus" and "Cap" Wallis, went out on a little trouble-hunting expedition by themselves. All four had things coming their way for a while, trying to shoot up the first- and second-line enemy trenches. They silenced a few machine-gun and anti-aircraft batteries, but Lambert's gasoline tank was punctured in about fifteen places by machine-gun bullets, and the wings and fuselage were shot full of holes. They managed to make our side of the lines all right, but what was left was a pure salvage job. Captain Wallis had his cheek cut open by a machine-gun bullet. Schaffner on the other hand had better luck, escaping with a few bullet holes in his wings and a piece nicked out of the prop.

Maury Hill was the second on the promoted list, leaving for Tours this same evening. Cook taking his place as leader of the third flight. On the 12th Major Reynolds led over a formation to try out the suggestion that we drop an occasional bomb on the other side. His ship was the only one carrying bombs, and of the four dropped over Thiaucourt, three registered direct hits. Lambert and Baker went over as protection. On the way back four *Pfalz* scouts jumped the formation and during the fight Baker, one of the gamest observers that ever served his country, was shot through the abdomen. As soon as Lambert could get back to the field. Baker was rushed to a hospital, where hopes were at first held out for his recovery, but the next day, in spite of a transfusion of blood, it was seen that the wound was fatal, and he died on the 15th.

In the meantime Schaffner had also been given a squadron of his own, and "Vic" Strahm succeeded to his position as leader of the second flight.

Lambert had been assigned one of the new observers, Mangan, and a few hours before Baker's funeral on the 15th, their motor quit cold over Metz just as they were starting on a photographic mission. "Jesus" at once turned, luckily with the wind at his back, and, followed by six Boches, headed for the nearest point of the lines. Mangan kept shooting continuously, firing over three hundred rounds of ammunition, and managed to keep the Boches from getting too close until a third-flight mission came in sight, and the enemy, suspecting reinforcements, turned back toward their home grounds at Frescaty. Lambert finally managed to cross the lines at about 800 metres elevation, but landing places around Pont-a-Mousson are scarce, and "Jesus" had his third crash in two days. That evening he was ordered by the major to take a three days' rest to get his mind off the war for a while.

On the 16th another "Back Area" friend arrived in the person of 2nd Lt. Harold J. Hotton, and Fleck was replaced by 2nd Lt. Robert T. Boyd. H-H-H-Hugh Fontaine left at the same time, having finally been transferred to chasse, for which he had applied some time previously.

During the rest of the month fairly continuous good weather kept everybody on the move, and before the end of August the sector was photographed over practically every square foot, and the squadron, both pilots and observers, had become a veteran outfit. Nearly every mission that went over came back reporting a combat, but the Boches seemed to bear charmed lives; it seemed almost impossible to bring them down, no matter how many rounds of tracers entered their machines. The squadron was further reinforced with both pilots and observers in preparation for the coming offensive, of which rumours were already starting to fly around. Second Lieutenants Richard S. Jannopoulo and Raymond R. Sebring reported on the 22nd, Capt. Abraham Tabachnik on the 23rd, and 2nd Lts. John W. Schricker and John S. Richardson on the 26th as observers. While to the pilots roster were added the names of 1st Lt. Leon W. Powell and 1st Lt. William F. Baker, who arrived on the 26th. Major Martin F. Scanlon, J. M. A., was temporarily assigned to us on the 26th.

A new army observation squadron, the 24th, moved in on the 23rd to help us, but their ships did not begin to arrive until some time after, and then all the pilots had to start learning to fly Salmsons. First Lieutenant Harry Miller, formerly of the 1st Aero Squadron, was in command, but on Sept. 4th the news came through that he was to be replaced by Maury Hill, and that another 91st man, "Quiet" Cousins, Maury's old observer, would go to the 24th as operations officer. Henderson left on the 27th.

September opened with a foretaste of what was to come. On the 22nd, during a photographic mission over Metz, the fighting second flight again ran into a flock of Boches, and in a hot "dog-fight", which lasted all the way back to the lines, brought down three enemy planes, which, however, were never confirmed, as they fell too far back to be observed. Strahm and "Cap" Wallis, Lambert and Mangan, "Pep" Fos-

"Quiet" Cousins and Maury Hill.

ter and Perry, and Hughey and Roper, were the four teams that took part in this encounter with a total of twelve enemy machines. None of our planes was badly shot up, but the Boches certainly learned something about the difficulty of bringing down a Salmson.

"Pep" Foster had his oft-repeated wish that he might "get in lots of time over the lines" granted on the 4th, when the same quartet got in hot water again. On this occasion three enemy ships attacked the formation and immediately closed in. One of them dove on Foster's machine and shot Sebring, his observer, killing him instantly. To try to shake the Boches, "Pep" went into a dive, with the enemy on his tail. Hughey followed the pair down, and after firing a few bursts with his front gun, set the enemy on fire. "Vic" dove on another machine, and this one, too, went down in flames. This seemed to scare the third, as he made off for home. Foster put his ship into a spiral, and was finally seen to land in enemy territory.

On the 5th, Major Reynolds announced that he had been placed in command of the 1st Army observation Group, which was to be composed of the 91st, 24th, and 9th squadrons. Cook was announced at the same time as C. O. of the 91st while Kenneson and Perry went to the 9th squadron to do night observation work. Stone, Downing, and Jervey became engineering officer, supply officer, and armament officer, respectively, of the group, and Hammond left the first flight to become group adjutant, Terry became group intelligence officer and Snyder group operations officer on the 11th.

Another of the original teams was lost on the 7th, when during a combat over Conflans between three ships of the first flight and four Fokkers, "Al" Lawson and his observer Verwohlt were forced to land in enemy territory. Word was later received that Verwohlt had been shot through the leg. Three new pilots reported for duty on the 8th, 2nd Lts. Paul D. Coles, Edward K. Delana, and Samuel G. Frierson.

The work that had been going on since our arrival on the front was now about completed. The whole sector had been photographed and re-photographed at intervals of every two weeks, while dumps, strategic points, and all information of value to an attacking army had been noted and tabulated. On the 11th of September came the news that the squadron had been awaiting for some time, and in the evening the major announced to us that the first all-American push was to start the next morning with a terrific artillery preparation, followed by the doughboys' rush over the top at daybreak in an attempt to wipe out the famous St. Mihiel salient. The news was succeeded by one of our well-known revival meetings around the piano. Rev. Van Heuvel leading in prayer and Deacon Diekema tickling the ivories. All night long the big guns kept up their work, and the first missions over in the morning reported that the whole front from Pont-a-Mousson to St. Mihiel was on fire.

Worse flying weather can hardly be imagined than that in which we flew during the 12th, 13th, and 14th, the three main days of the attack, but missions left, and returned with their information, on a regular schedule, interrupted only by an occasional shower of driving rain. Missions were constantly carried out at altitudes of from fifty to one hundred meters far over the enemy lines in an endeavour to get the information asked for, and even darkness did not stop the flying, missions searching for enemy batteries going out on the evenings of the 12th and 13th and returning by the aid of flares long after dark. On account of the low clouds it was almost impossible to keep formations together, but in every case when a ship became separated from the others, it went over the course, and performed the mission, most of the time flying just under the clouds, and zooming back into them whenever the fire from the ground became too hot or whenever the enemy chasse attacked.

On the 13th Diekema and Hammond flew to Mars la Tour, then over to Gorze, and back to Chambley, at no time being over one hundred metres up. At the same time Strahm and "Cap" Wallis, while on a mission southeast of Metz, were attacked by a Fokker at about eight hundred meters altitude. About seventy-five rounds from "Cap" Wallis's pair of Lewis guns, however, sufficed, and the enemy machine crashed near Orly Ferme, making the second official Boche for this team.

The operations of the 14th cost the squadron another of the old teams. Paul Hughey and Roper went out on a visual mission early in the morning, and five months passed without word of them. The antis on this day gave one of the new men. Coles, a chance to distinguish himself. One of the Archie bursts tore off half of both lower wings, but although the ship became almost unmanageable. Coles succeeding in bringing it back to the field and making a good landing. For his first trip over the lines his coolness was remarkable, his first words on landing being, "How long will if take to put on another pair of wings? I like to fly that boat, she handles so well." Strahm and Wallis had a combat with six red-nosed *Pfalzes*, and "Cap'n Abe" Tabachnik had his machine-guns shot out of his hands during another fight. While

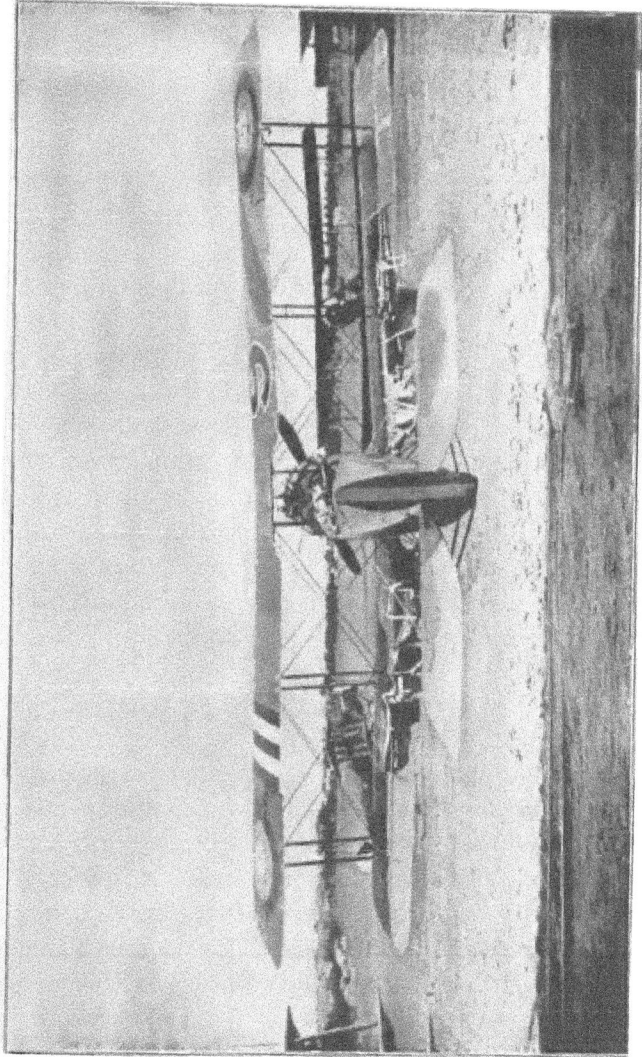

No. 9 AFTER COLES' FIRST TRIP

"Mose" Guilbert and Tom Jervey fought off eighteen Fokkers in a running fight all the way from Conflans to St. Mihiel.

Two more official Boches were added to the squadron list on the 15th. The first flight started out on a photographic mission from Gorze north, but had barely started taking pictures, when the formation of four was attacked by six *Pfalz* scouts. Two of them dove for Coles's ship, which was flying as protection in the rear, and at the first burst a machine-gun bullet pierced his neck, forcing him to make for the lines, as he wanted to land safely before he fainted from loss of blood. The other three jumped Kenney's machine, but his observer, Badham, who had just straightened up in the cockpit from taking pictures, poured a few bursts into one of the enemy machines, sending it down in flames. Kenney's ship was badly shot up, one of the elevators being almost off, so he turned back toward the field. In spite of thus losing the rest of the flight, "Diek" and Hammond climbed back to regain the altitude lost during the combat and continued on their mission. Which they accomplished without further attack, although several formations of enemy ships were seen around them.

At almost the same time the second flight encountered six more *Pfalzes* just south of Briey, and during the combat one of the opposing planes was brought down by a new man, Schricker, who was flying in the rear seat of the ship piloted by Powell, himself a new man. That evening the doctors at the hospital where Coles had been taken gave out the welcome news that he would probably be out of the game only about six weeks.

During the afternoon a mission was called for to go on a visual reconnaissance to Diedenhofen (Thionville). Major Scanlon volunteered, as every other pilot was on some other mission at the time, taking "Shorty" Lawson, still weak from his wound but anxious to work, as his observer. They penetrated enemy territory for a distance of seventy-five kilometres, constantly under Archie fire except when the Boches appeared, when the Salmson would dive in a friendly cloud, emerging as soon as it had shaken off the pursuit. The flight was not only a spectacular one, but much valuable information was brought back.

Heavy rain put an end to our flying the next day, and in the evening we received word that the drive was off until further orders. To relieve the tension resulting from the preceding weeks the flights were each given two days leave. which was of course spent in Nancy. Major Scanlon's impersonation of a horse proved to be the star act in a bill

Photo section No. 2

crowded with novelties, and Vic's debate with a certain G. H. Q. major, followed by an unaccountable advocacy of the prohibition cause, was another feature.

Schaffner in the meantime had heard that a drive was going on and had borrowed a Spad for the occasion from the field at Is-sur-Til, where his new squadron was assembling. He arrived at Gondreville on the 17th, and, much disgusted when he learned that the drive was off, told the crowd to "go ahead and play with" his Spad. During one of these trials, on the 18th, Guilbert unfortunately crashed, breaking his arm, putting "Mose" out of the flying game until the 8th of November. From Sept. 25th to that date, however, he acted as liaison officer at Air Service Headquarters of the IVth French Army.

"Photo" was transferred to the 1st Corps Observation Group on the 18th, 2nd Lt. William A. Barnhill taking his place as photographic officer. At the same time 1st Lt. Sumner Carlisle arrived as squadron supply officer. On the 20th orders came to pack up and move over to Vavincourt, (about six kilometres north of Bar-le-Duc), from which field we were to work over the Argonne-Meuse sector during the second great American drive, which was to start soon. The last ship was ferried over by the 22nd, and the next day the first missions were sent over the new sector. Schaff had prolonged his "visit" and managed to get over the lines with his old flight on two different occasions before an urgent telegram recalled him to his squadron on the 25th.

The attack on the Argonne-Meuse front began on the 26th, and the first day's operations cost us another of the old teams, when "Ash" Kelty and Lowry were killed by a direct hit of anti-aircraft fire. Kelty had been flight leader of the third flight since Cook had taken command of the squadron, and everyone had come to realise how valuable he was, while Lowry was recognised as one of the best observers in the squadron. Their loss was keenly felt, especially as we now had only eight teams working, for we had not yet received replacements for the heavy losses suffered during the past month. Pilots and observers, however, made two and sometimes three flights a day, and the work of photographing and collecting information to aid the drive Went on without interruption.

The squadron had received four new observers, 1st Lts. Asa N. Duncan, John B. Pope, Robert G. Scott, and John H. Whitaker, on the 25th, and three more joined the ranks on the 27th, 1st Lts. George B. Merrill and Samuel P. Fay, and 2nd Lt. William J. Moran; but the real shortage was in pilots, and for the next two weeks they went through

"The Queen of the Air"

the hardest work they had experienced to date.

It was on the 27th also that the squadron lost the services of Jannopoulo as an observer for the rest of the war. Three of our planes, manned by Cook and Lawson, Baker and Jannopoulo, and Van Heuvel and Hammond, were attacked while on a photographic mission over Damvillers by six Fokkers, who closed in with a rush, their leading ship being met with a burst of concentrated fire which sent it whirling down in flames. The enemy formation then drew off, but not before "Jap" had received a bullet in his chest which missed his heart by a matter of a inch or so. Baker, his pilot, at once left the formation and headed for Souilly, to get him as quickly as possible to the hospital there.

Another old 91st pilot took over the command of a squadron on Oct. 2nd, when Kenneson replaced 1st Lt. T. A. Box, formerly of the 88th, as C. O, of the 9th night observation squadron. Which had been attached to the 91st and 24th, forming the 1st Army Observation Group.

Frierson and Scott entered the list of casualties on the 5th. They were over on a mission with Lambert and Mangan, flying above the clouds, but the visibility being too poor to get the desired information, they dove through. After Lambert lost sight of Frierson's ship in the clouds he was not seen again. The only news we received was from one of the American pursuit pilots, who reported a lone allied plane being chased north by an enemy patrol of about fifteen enemy machines, the time and place coinciding almost exactly with that of the missing pair when last seen. "Johnny" Wise left us on the 6th.

By this time, with the American forces pressing the enemy on all points between the Argonne and the Meuse, the Boches had concentrated practically all their available planes from Mezieres to Metz to prevent our getting information about their back areas. The weather was continuing fair, and every flight across the lines meant at least one combat before the mission was over. The enemy attacked without the care that he had displayed on the Toul sector, and in consequence, during the coming month, we brought down a number of enemy planes far out of proportion to what might be expected of an observation squadron.

On the 9th one of our formations of three ships was attacked by fourteen Fokkers in the neighbourhood of Jametz, and after a fierce combat, in which we were finally driven from our course, and which lasted practically all the way back to Verdun, three enemy planes were brought down, with all three of our ships pretty well shot up, although none of the pilots or observers was hit. Kenney and Duncan, Delana and Merrill, and Chamberlin and Sieper, were the teams officially credited with the destruction of the enemy planes.

Major Reynolds on the following day was credited with the destruction of his first Boche. With Hammond as observer he was attacked by four enemy planes, but again the twin Lewis guns won, and the enemy leader went into a nosedive, finally crashing, his fall being confirmed by the American balloon observers.

Shorty Lawson left the squadron on the 14th to go back to the States as instructor. Bill Badham taking his place as operations officer. At the same time we were directed by Air Service Headquarters to furnish a flight to do post of command work at low altitudes over the front lines, operating from Souilly, so accordingly four teams from the second flight were sent up the headquarters on the 16th and started work.

On the 10th our shortage of pilots was relieved when three new names were added to the roster, 2nd Lts. Harold S. Watson, Roy J. Wasson, and Merle R. Husted. The following day 1st Lts. Earle Houghton, Norfleet E. Armstrong, and Orton F. Hoel also began their duties as pilots. On the 16th 2nd Lt. James D. Adams arrived, bringing up the list to its full strength. The complement of observers had already been filled up on the 9th by the arrival of 1st Lts. Alvin C. Kincaid, James E. Ainslie, and Henry E. Bash.

One of the newly-arrived pilots, Watson, and his observer Merrill, crashed on the 18th soon after taking off from the field. Just what caused if is not known, but unfortunately Watson was instantly killed and Merrill badly injured, so that he was out of the game for the duration of the war. On the same day Maury Hill, C. O. of the 24th, received his captaincy, the name of another old 91st man, Herbert Schaffner, now in command of the 85th squadron, being on the same order.

Our first casualty on the post of command work came on the 21st, when Adams and Bash were reported missing. From information later received by our intelligence department we learned that they had been forced to land behind the German lines and had been made, prisoners.

The enemy patrols had during the past few days been further increased, and on the 23rd every flight that went over the lines encountered huge mass formations of Fokkers and *Pfalzes*, numbering between forty and sixty pursuit machines. During one of the numerous combats that took place in the course of the day. Cook and Badham, Doug and Hammond, and Houghton and Fay were credited with bringing down one Fokker in flames and one *Pfalz* out of control. All of our planes were badly shot up, and Houghton was wounded in the hip, putting another pilot out of the game for the duration of the war.

The next day another pilot, Baker, had to leave the squadron permanently. A leaky valve had developed in his heart, so Doc Gray pulled him off the flying list, and he was later assigned to ground service. Johnny Snyder left us on the 25th to go to Tours for instruction as a pilot, Cap Wallis taking his place as group operations officer.

Another of the new pilots, Armstrong, was fatally injured on the 28th, when he crashed on his way to our airdrome from a forced landing. Private J. B. Irvin, who was in the back seat, was slightly injured. Cook and Badham added to their list of enemy planes destroyed on the same date when they brought down a Fokker which attacked them over the lines while they were on a visual mission. The enemy machine was reported by the American balloon observers as falling in flames.

Major Reynolds was officially credited with his second Boche on the 29th. Two of our planes were attacked by five *Pfalz* scouts over Grandpre, but our concentration of fire drove one of them down in flames, and the others, after following our formation over the lines a short distance, gave up the pursuit. The major and Hammond, and Cook and Badham, were the two teams who took part in the combat. The squadron was engaged in five different combats during the day, but the others were without result, so far as is known.

The 30th was a big day for the 91st. In all, the squadron exposed 234 plates over the enemy lines, and fought five combats, during which two enemy ships were brought down. "The flying ordnance officer", Tom Jervey, with Vic Strahm, took pictures for the first time, snapping thirty-six in all, of which thirty-four were good, while Professor Strahm's boy Victor, not wishing to have his observer get too much credit, shot down an enemy Rumpler which seemed to resent their presence in that locality. Lambert and Pope were acting as protection for Vic and Tom, and soon after the Rumpler had dropped, "Jesus" dove on a formation of three *Pfalzes* which were trying to prevent the mission from returning, and in the combat which followed sent one of them down out of control. The enemy plane crashed just south of Stenay.

TOM AND VIC.

The month of October closed for the squadron in a blaze of glory. During the day a great number of important missions were carried out in spite of constant attacks by the enemy patrols. Six combats were engaged in, and two more enemy machines added to our list. Strahm and Jervey, and Lambert and Pope, started to take a photographic mission between Montmedy and Longuyon, when they were jumped by fourteen Fokkers. A whirlwind combat was the result, in which two enemy machines went down, one in flames, the other in a straight nose-dive. The formation had been driven back off the course during the fight, and here Lambert turned back home, as his ship had been too badly shot up to continue on the course. Although Tom and Vic had only a hundred rounds of ammunition left, they turned back and finished their mission. First Lieutenants Harry C Atkins and Robert M. Barnett joined the squadron as observers on the same day.

On the 3rd of November Cook and Strahm put on their double bars, their captaincies having come through dated November 1st.

Bad weather put an end to the "Boche-getting" for a few days, but on the 4th Diek and Sieper turned in the surprising total of three Boches brought down during a single flight. Sieper got the first when five enemy ships turned them off their course, and on returning to complete the mission Diek dove on a formation of six ships coming up to attack and brought down one of them. Diek then turned back home, but in the meantime Sieper had sent another down in flames.

Strahm and Jervey on the same day, while on a long-distance visual, were attacked by a new method, five biplace fighters jumping them near Conflans. Vic brought the ship back with twenty-five holes in the wings and fuselage, and the added information that Tom had brought down another Boche, which was later confirmed officially.

From the 3rd to the 9th a number of replacements arrived to fill up vacancies. The following reported as pilots: 1st Lts. Russell Graham and Bernard G. Westover; 2nd Lts. Arthur H. Weisbach, French Kirby, Louis M. Bruch, Kirtly Jones, Raymond W. Sweeney, and Harold S. Thorne. The observers Were; 1st Lts. Lyman T. Burgess, John B. Copeland, John C. Orr, and Victor H. Withstandley; 2nd Lts. William A. White, Paul C. Wienges, Arthur M. Farnsworth, Linus E. Russell, Lloyd A. Ruth, George W. Mayer, and Barclay F. Bowman.

Bruch and White, and Thorne and Farnsworth, crossed the lines while on post of command work with the first flight at Souilly during the last few days of the war, but the others, including 2nd Lt. Lloyd A. Ruth of Minneapolis, did not get a chance to get over before the war ended.

Pop Seymour left us on the 9th, going to Tours to teach observers the gentle art of watching for Boches while taking pictures.

On the 10th Bryan, Sieper, Powell, and Schricker were detailed to the 2nd Army to form the nucleus of a new squadron in process of formation, and left for Toul, where they discovered that they would be under the command of an old 91st pilot, Captain Herbert A. Schaffner of the 8th Squadron.

Major Reynolds' long deserved promotion to lieutenant-colonel came through on the 8th, and the following evening a dinner was given him by the officers of his old squadron. Sutherland saved the day by his eleventh-hour arrival from Chalons, where he had been "on official business". The evening passed with a warm glow of sociability and toasts to all present. The piano was subjected to a severe strain toward the close of the celebration, Vic pouring forth a composition all his own while Diek, who had come down from Souilly for the occasion, played an accompaniment. Hammond's captaincy came through at the same time, while another old 91st observer. Cousins, now operations officer of the 24th, was on the same list. Diek's captaincy arrived the following day dated the 9th.

On the 10th came our final casualty, Bruch and White failing to return from a post of command mission of Souilly. They started out over Stenay, and evidently became lost, as the fog was fairly thick and the clouds were low. The loss was especially unfortunate as on the following day at 11 o'clock hostilities ceased, according to the terms of the armistice.

When it was evident that the armistice was a question of days only, several enterprising spirits, among whom the major and Hammond should be mentioned, conceived the brilliant idea of a peace pool, little realising that by the time the peace treaties were signed we'd be grey-headed or in our graves. George Kenney drew up a most convincing circular, and the shares were rapidly bought up by the officers of the three squadrons in the group, under the following plan: ninety shares were to be sold, their par value 100 *francs*, the names of the men holding them to be drawn by lot and assigned as they were drawn to the different days of the month, three to each day, from the 1st to the 30th, inclusive.

The three men who have the day of the month on which the treaties of peace are finally signed will divide the nine thousand *francs*, making something over five hundred dollars per man. If the treaties

DUN-SUR-MEUSE, TAKEN NOV. 2ND, 1918, ALT. 1100 METRES, HUS-
TED PILOT, MORAN, OBSERVER

are signed on the 31st, the pool is a "dud", and the fund goes to pay expenses at the reunion of the first squadron in the group to hold one—meaning the 91st, Each holder of a share of stock received a certificate, a photographic reproduction of the original which is the property of Lt. Col. Reynolds, on which, above the wording in heavy letters, appear the insignias of the three squadrons concerned.

The first event of importance following the armistice was the dinner on Nov. 13th, given in one of the hangars by the men to celebrate the first anniversary of the squadron's arrival in France. Except for the absence of the major, "Ham", "Doug", and one or two others, who were in Paris—the first two *en route* to Nice on a well-earned leave—the party was complete. An elaborate dinner, with a menu-card and program drawn up by the photo section as only it can do things of the kind, was followed by not too many speeches. Lieutenant Ripley acted as master of ceremonies, and his impassioned and dramatic recital of the squadron's journey to France, with references to the various rest camps, will dwell long in our memories. Tom Jervey's proposal to organise a squadron to fight prohibition, on our return to the States, met with wild approval.

Following the speeches there was a vaudeville show in which the singing of the quartet and Miner's playing of the Hawaiian guitar seemed to make the biggest hits. When the evening was ended all agreed that the celebration had been fully up to 91st standards.

During the first few days after the armistice, all sorts of rumours were floating around, mostly concerned with when we were going home, until it was learned that the squadron was to be "honoured" by forming part of the Army of Occupation. During these days the squadron lived along in pretty much the same old groove, the only events to relieve the monotony being a show or two at the "Y", where Mr. Thomas G, Trenchard, who had joined the group on Nov. 1st, was making a name for himself as one of the best of all "Y' secretaries. On the 14th 1st Lt. Nelson Fell reported as intelligence officer, and 2nd Lt. Clyde Young as radio officer.

On the 21st the first move of the journey into Germany was made, a jump of sixty miles or more from Vavincourt to a former German airdrome at Preutin, a village which can best be located as roughly twenty-five miles directly north-west of Metz. No trouble was experienced in getting all the planes moved, as the day on which the squadron left Vavincourt was beautifully clear. As a field occupied by the Boches until a very short time before, Preutin was in many ways

"Doug."

interesting. A number of Fokkers and other plane, wrecked by our infantry on their passage through, were on the field, the town was full of evidences of German occupation, and the *château* where most of the officers were billeted had been occupied by the officers of the German squadrons, and was one more proof that the Boches "know how to live". The people of the village had many stories about the Germans and their four years in the place, and of the fighting for Verdun, The principal event of the squadron's stay there was Thanksgiving Day, memorable mainly for the fine dinner with which officers and men celebrated—corned Wilhelm, called turkey in honour of the day, canned corn, canned tomatoes, canned everything. A saving feature of the stay at Preutin was our nearness to Metz and Luxembourg, both cities that all were anxious to visit, and to which parties went daily. Capt. Cyrus P. Brown Jr., joined the squadron as observer on Dec. 1st.

The "Major" brought a Cadillac-full of the old crowd over from Vavincourt one afternoon on a farewell visit before their return to the States—"Ham", Downing, "Jimmy" Wallis, Maury Hill, Cousins, and Coles, who had just been discharged from the hospital. They brought the news that Distinguished Service Crosses had been awarded to thirteen of the officers in, or formerly in, the 91st—Lt. Col. Reynolds, Badham, Cook, Cousins, Diekema, Douglass, Hammond, Jervey, Kenney, Lambert, Snyder, Strahm, and Wallis—and that the ceremony of decoration would take place in the near future. At the same time if was learned that the *Croix de Guerre* with a palm had been awarded to Bender, Guilbert, and Van Heuvel, and posthumously to Hirth. The D. S. C. was subsequently awarded to the following former members of the squadron: Fontaine, Maury Hill and "Shorty" Lawson.

Kenney, as transportation officer, distinguished himself while at Preutin by putting into commission an enormous Boche tractor which he and his "gang" found in a nearby village where if had been abandoned by the Germans. It was a big day when it was driven up to the truck park (?) at Preutin with a half-dozen trailers in which, according to Kenney, all the squadron property was to be transported, on our next move, in one haul. During the rest of our stay at Preutin the tractor was enormously useful, principally in pulling the 91st's Packard trucks out of the way when they were stuck in the mud.

On Dec. 2nd orders came to move on to Treves, or Trier, on the Moselle, about sixty miles from Preutin. Diek and Lambert left in their Salmsons on the receipt of the news, Wickins and an advance

"DIEK."

detail from the mess following them in a light truck. That was on Monday afternoon, and until the next Friday it was impossible, owing to weather conditions, for a plane to leave the field. The work of moving the squadron nevertheless went on, no easy job, as it was a two-day haul. As a through train, the tractor fell down on the job. Hauling half a dozen trailers, all marked "91st Aero Squadron" in large white letters, it burned out a crankshaft-bearing a few miles from Preutin, and had to be abandoned, while the contents of the trailers were loaded into the more prosaic but always reliable Packards.

On the Saturday following Diek's and Lambert's departure, "Doug", "Van", and "Vic", wearied of waiting for the weather to clear, and made desperate by the prospect of spending any more time in "this Godforsaken hole", as everyone referred to it, took off, in spite of the low clouds. They made Treves, after a wild ride in which they dodged the smoke-stacks suddenly looming up through the fog, flew over the Moselle at less than fifty meters, and did everything that one ordinarily never does. Weather conditions made it impossible for any other ships to leave the field until eight days later. The inconvenience of having part of the squadron at one place and part at another, and the boredom of the men waiting at Preutin for the weather to clear, will never be forgotten. If was not until the day before Christmas, three weeks after the squadron first moved from Preutin, that the last machine was flown to Treves and the transportation, mess, and hangar men could rejoin the squadron.

It was at Treves that we had our first opportunity to fly the Boche machines turned over to the Allies, and taking rides in the Fokker or the *Pfalz* became a popular sport, with an occasional jaunt in a Hannover or a Halberstadt. On the 20th came an honour which we should have been glad to forego, when "Diek" was made C. O. of the 9th, in place of Kenneson, who was relieved to go back to the States. The next day we welcomed old Tom Jervey back to the fold; with everyone else on his way back to the States, the group had no charms for him. It was while we were at Treves that Miss Blanche Fenton and Miss Enid Allen arrived to work in the "Y", and with true heroism came occasionally to our mess.

Christmas Day we spent at Treves, our second Christmas in Europe, and not by any means a bad day. No one had such home comforts as Christmas stockings, but the atmosphere at the dinner given in the hangar by the men at two o'clock, to which all the officers originally in the squadron were invited, was cheerful if not warm. The menu was excellent, and the tree in the centre of the hangar, decorated as they are at home, made everyone happy (or homesick, as the case might be), just to look at it. In the evening the officers had their dinner, with Miss Fenton, Miss Allen, Mr. Trenchard, and his assistant, Mr. Hull, as guests, with a free (decorations in part swiped from the other) and presents for everyone. Some, such as the ticket to the States for poor homesick Boyd, the bottle of milk for Mike Delana, and for Stone (of course) a fragment of the bomb that shook his inkwell, made a decided hit.

There is little else to record of our stay in Treves except the football game with the 9th squadron. The score was a 0 to 0 tie, but all agreed that if was really a victory for the 91st; "Chick" Broderick's ragging between the halves, with such remarks as "It takes the 9th and the 1st to make the 91st", and "It's a disgrace for a fine officer like Captain Diekema to have to command such a bunch as you", being distinctly entitled to a decision.

Boyd's long-expected and longed-for orders to go home came just before we left Treves, and others who left the squadron while it was there were Chamberlin, Copeland, Jones, Mangan, Stone, Burgess and Westover.

New Year's Day was also spent at Treves, and orders for the move to Coblenz came in the afternoon. Doug and Weisbach in Salmsons and Cook in his Spad left the next morning. Following their arrival at Coblenz, orders came for the rest to stay at Treves until more hangars had been put up on the Coblenz field. Two days later, Saturday, Jan. 4th, word was received to ferry up the rest of the planes, and all that started got through a bumpy ride without incident. The pilots returned to Treves by train, and Monday the rest of the planes were flown up. What might have been a serious accident occurred when a Liberty, landing at Treves, ran into Graham in a Fokker, taxiing out to take off. The Liberty's prop sliced the fuselage in two directly behind Graham's seat, and rolled the Fokker over and over; but except for a wrenched knee Graham emerged unhurt.

On our arrival at Coblenz we found that the 91st, 94th, and 12th Squadrons were to occupy Fort Alexander, on the steep hill back of the city. The field was a former parade ground, and the work of putting up hangars was still in progress. Under the command of Major H. B. Anderson, C. O. of the 4th Corps Observation Group, formerly commanding the 88th Squadron, and an old friend of the 91st, all three squadrons quickly settled down to the daily routine.

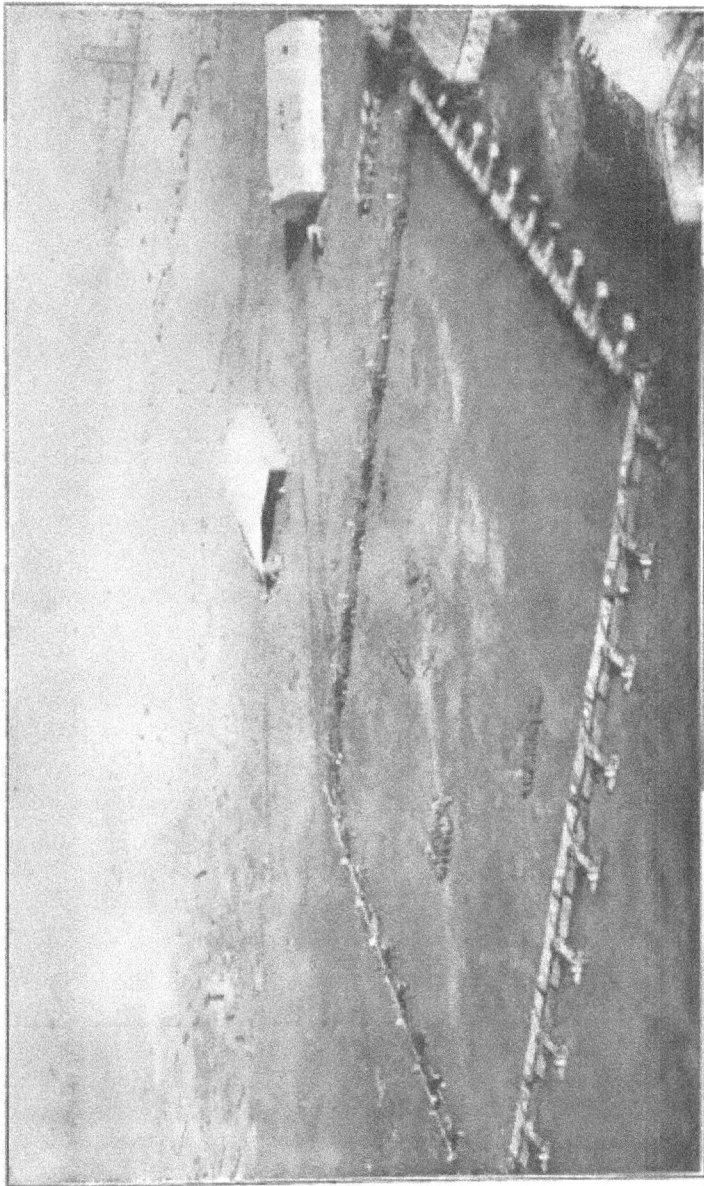

DECORATION CEREMONY JAN 10TH, 1919

On Jan. 10th Brigadier-General William Mitchell, in an impressive ceremony, decorated the officers to whom the D. S. C.'s had been awarded some time previously, Diek coming up from Treves in a Breguet to receive his. After the ceremony of decoration. General Mitchell, who was to leave for the States in a few days, made a short farewell address, in which he paid a tribute to the work of the 91st, saying "No squadron ever performed such reconnaissances as you have, working fifty kilometres behind the lines, and getting away with it."

The next day the general came to the airdrome with the Prince of Wales, whom he took up in his bi-place Spad. After the flight, all the officers on the field were called together and presented individually to the prince by Major Anderson.

The 91st at last gave its much talked-of dance on Monday, Jan. 13th, in the officers' mess. The refreshments held out to the end, and the celebration was wound up by a supper of venison steaks from 1.30 to 2.30 a.m.

On the 15th, Rip was detached from the squadron and assigned to G. H Q. in Coblenz as adjutant to Lt. Col. Harold Fowler, who had succeeded Gen. Mitchell as Chief of Air Service, 3rd Army, Bill Moran taking Rip's place as squadron adjutant. On the 22nd Bill Badham and Tabachnik left for Colombey-les-Belles, with hopes of being sent home from there, both of them expecting to be married shortly after their arrival in the States.

In the week ending on the 18th the squadron was saddened by the deaths in the hospital, from influenza, of three men: Privates Willard R. Augustus, and Charles F. Chatelle, and Sergeant Bryant F. Van Kirk, who had been in the 1st Aero Squadron on the Border, and had therefore been in the service longer than any other man in the squadron. At the same time we learned of Kenneson's death from the same cause in Paris on Jan. 10th, while on his way home.

In the meantime, Kenney had made two trips to Paris on "official business", and came back with news from all our missing pilots and observers except Hughey and Roper.

Battle and Williamson had dropped within a few hundred yards of the Boche front line trenches near Flirey. "Bat" had tried to escape three times, but finally had to wait for the end of the war before leaving his German home. Both left for the States during the latter part of January.

Mayes had been sent home soon after the armistice, still suffering from wounds received in his combat with seven Fokkers near Thiau-

Captain Everett R. Cook, commanding officer

court.

"Pep" Foster recounted a wonderful tale. When Sebring was killed a few stray bullets bumped "Pep" on the head and knocked him unconscious. He finally came to on the ground underneath the wreck of his plane, and on emerging from his hiding place was immediately made prisoner and taken to Jarny, where he shared the same room with an R. F. C. pilot captured a few days before. Some days later the two prisoners saw a formation over their heads and immediately made a bet of fifty *marks*, "Pep" wagering that the 91st was the only squadron that ever flew that far back, while the Englishman made a similar claim about his daylight bombing outfit. Shortly after the argument, "Al" Lawson was brought into the prison and "Pep" immediately claimed the coin. "Al's" observer, Verwohlt, had been shot in the knee with an explosive bullet and had lost a leg. All three returned home early in 1919.

Frierson had been brought down near Clery-le-Petit after a furious combat with fifteen Fokkers, one of which Frierson had brought down with his front gun. Scott had been killed before a bullet in the motor forced Frierson to land, with a wound in his leg. While setting the ship on fire he was shot twice more and was then backed up against a wall with a firing squad in front of him. A German officer, wishing to question him about the American Air Service, rescued him just in time. Frierson's complete ignorance regarding everything of importance "foxed" the officer completely. The Germans thought Sam was "holding out", but as far as is known the thousands of *marks'* worth of champagne devoted to the cause never brought forth information enough to shorten the war. Frierson rejoined the squadron at Coblenz on the 16th of February.

Kenney on both trips visited Bash in the hospital at Toul, where he was recovering from eleven bullet wounds and a burned foot received when he and Adams were brought down by six Fokkers north of Brieulles. They were doing Post of Command work when they were surprised by the enemy. The tank caught on fire, but Bash, by putting his foot over the hole in the tank, managed to keep the flames from spreading, and although he was badly burned enabled Adams to land the machine safely. Lack of care on the part of the Germans nearly cost Bash his life, but when seen at Toul he was rapidly recovering. Adams, who was unhurt, left for home during January.

The graves of Bruch and White were found at Inor-sur-Meuse, and it was learned from the French villagers there that the plane had been brought down by machine gun fire from the ground.

Cook had also made an official visit to Paris, and returned with the news that the D. S. C. had been awarded posthumously to "Ash" Kelty and Lowry.

Tuesday afternoon, Feb. 18th, saw the squadron, with a band from the 4th Air Park, drawn up on the field in front of a line of Salmsons and German planes to receive from the hand of Lt. Col. Fowler the Letters of Merit awarded by the Air Service Commander, 1st Army, and by the C. O. of the squadron. Letters were awarded to the following officers and men: From the Air Service Commander, 1st Army: Capt. Tabachnik, 1st Lts. Duncan, Fay, Houghton, Kincaid, Pope, Seymour, Verwohlt, and Whitaker; 2nd Lts. Coles, Delana, Husted, Moran, and Wasson; Master Electrician Ray McAnally; Sgts. lst Cl. Matthews, Parady, Rowe, Snow, Souder, and Walker; Sgts. Easterbrook and Rike. From the Squadron Commander: lst Lts. Ainslie, Carlisle, Hoel, and Ripley; 2nd Lt. William A. Barnhill; Master Electricians Anderson and Schuelke; Sgts. 1st Cl. Carrigan, McAbee, and Wickins.

On the 19th, Private 1st Class Marion E. Moore, who had worked both in the intelligence office and the transportation department, died in the hospital from influenza, making the fourth death in the squadron since its arrival in Coblenz.

Major Anderson's tragic death on the 21st was an especially severe shock to the 91st because of our association with him during the long months spent at Amanty last year. He was buried from the post on Sunday the 23rd, the entire personnel of the 12th, 91st and 94th squadrons following his remains to the cemetery.

The 21st brought us other news of a tragic nature also. A letter was received from Capt. Zinn, of the Air Depot at Colombey-les-Belles, saying that he had found near Puxieux the graves of Hughey and Roper, missing in action on Sept. 14th, and of whom absolutely nothing had since been heard. The receipt of this information settled the last uncertainty regarding missing men, and brought the final casualty list up to a total of eleven men killed in action, two in accidents, thirteen wounded over the lines, and nine made prisoners.

Between the arrival of the squadron in Coblenz and the 22nd of February, the following officers joined the squadron to take the places of those who had returned to the States: 1st Lts. Thomas D. Howard and Charles F. Hudson, and 2nd Lts. Albert A. Allen Clarence A. Blum, Charles H. Cope, Donald E. Hardy, Klein L. Hooper, George S. Moran, Horatio A. Warren, and F. Vaughn Wilbur. The last week in Febru-

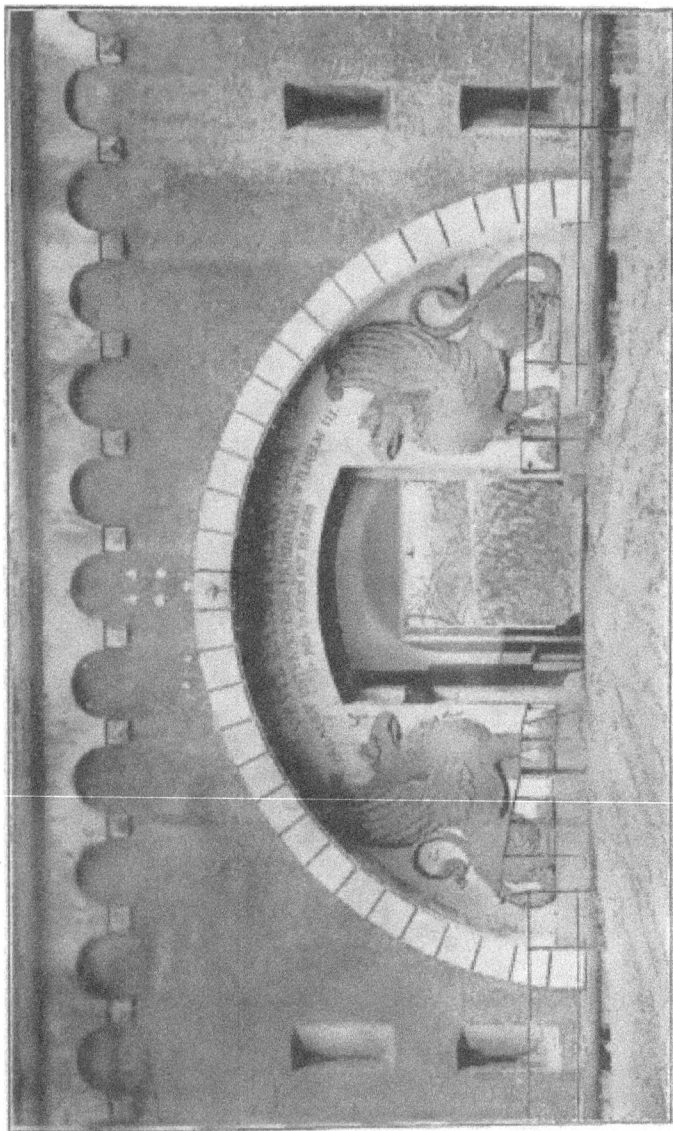

Entrance to Coblenz Airdrome

ary, "Doc" Gray received his promotion to captain, dated Jan. 27th.

It had been planned to hold a big reunion dinner on Washington's birthday to celebrate the first anniversary of the assignment of the original pilots to the squadron. Van Heuvel, however, was unable to get back from Paris in time, nor was "Hump" Bryan more successful in getting away from his duties in Toul as operations officer of the 2nd Army Air Service. "Diek" came up from his squadron in Treves, bringing Perry with him, and the celebration took the form of a quiet dinner at the officers' club at the casino, with Cook, Douglass, Guilbert, Jervey, Kenney, Lambert and Strahm as the others present, after which the old combination, Diek, Cookie, and Vic, once more tore off "Homesickness Blues", "Easy Riding Jockey", and "Balling the Jack", in this way the first year of the 91st's career as a completely organised squadron came to an end.

Summary of Work Performed by Squadron from May 29th to November 11th, 1918.

o o o

Destruction of Enemy Planes Confirmed : :	21
Number of Combats : : : : : : :	139
Number of Hours Beyond Enemy Lines : : :	1045
Distance in Kilometers Beyond Enemy Lines : :	25,380
Plates Exposed Beyond Enemy Lines : : :	4500
Successful Negatives : : : : : : :	3700
Prints Made From Negatives : : : :	143,233
Visual Reconnaissance Missions : : : :	252
Photographic Reconnaissance Missions : : :	108

o

Casualties.

Killed.

1st Lt. Norfleet E. Armstrong
1st Lt. Howard T. Baker
1st Lt. Paul H. Hughey
1st Lt. Asher E. Kelty
1st Lt. Kenyon Roper
1st Lt. Franz F. Schilling
1st Lt. Robert G. Scott
2nd Lt. Louis M. Bruch
2nd Lt. Frederick K. Hirth
2nd Lt. Francis B. Lowry
2nd Lt. Raymond R. Sebring
2nd Lt. Harold S. Watson
2nd Lt. William A. White

Wounded.

Capt. Walter R. Lawson
Capt. Abraham Tabachnik
Capt. James E. Wallis
1st Lt. Henry E. Bash
1st Lt. F. Vernon Foster
1st Lt. Earl Houghton
1st Lt. Alvan C. Kincaid
1st Lt. Howard G. Mayes
1st Lt. John W. Van Heuvel
1st Lt. Howard W. Verwohlt
2nd Lt. Paul D. Coles
2nd Lt. Samuel G. Frierson
2nd Lt. Richard S. Jannopoulo.

o

Prisoners.

Capt. Joseph F. Williamson
1st Lt. Henry E. Bash
1st Lt. Blanchard B. Battle
1st Lt. Frederick V. Foster
1st Lt. Alfred W. Lawson

1st Lt. Howard G. Mayes
1st Lt. Howard W. Verwohlt
2nd Lt. James D. Adams
2nd Lt. Samuel G. Frierson.

148

LIST OF OFFICERS.

Name	Address	Location
Adams, James D.	27 Salvatierra St.	Stanford University, C
Ainslie, James E.	4928 W. Pine Blvd.	St. Louis, Mo.
Allen, Albert A.	170 Northwestern Ave.	Detroit, Mich.
Armstrong, Norfleet E.	Killed in accident.	
Atkins, Harry C.		—
Badham, William T.	1221 Whittaker St.	Danbury, N. H.
Baker, Howard T.	Killed in action	Birmingham, Ala.
Baker, William F.	11 Holmes Ave.	
Barnett, Robert M.		Dorchester, Mass.
Barnhill, William A.		Franklin, Tenn.
Bash, Henry E.	1511 E. Berks	Philadelphia, Pa.
Battle, Blanchard B.	1005 N. Guilford St.	Huntington, Ind.
Bender, Walter	—	Columbus, Ga.
Blum, Clarence A.	8820 Fort Blvd.	El Paso, Tex.
Bowman, Barclay F.		Evansville, Ind.
Boyd, Robert T., Jr.	2053 Murray Ave.	Pittsburgh, Pa.
Brown, Cyrus P., Jr.	4806 Chestnut St.	Philadelphia, Pa.
Bruch, Louis M.	496 Portland Ave.	St. Paul, Minn.
Bryan, George H.	Killed in action	
Burgess, Lyman T.		Newport News, Va.
Carlisle, Sumner	2826 Nebraska St.	Sioux City, Iowa.
Chamberlin, Willard J.	—	Exeter, N. H.
Coles, Paul D.	1192 Franklin Ave.	Astoria, Ore.
Cook, Everett R.	4740 Fourth Ave., N. E.	Seattle, Wash.
Cope, Charles N.	1156 Linden Ave.	Memphis, Tenn.
Cope and, John B.	114 North High St.	Bethlehem, Pa.
Cousins, John W.		Jefferson, Wis.
Delana, Edward K.	1150 Whalley Ave.	New Haven, Conn.
Diekema, Willis A.	1215 Marquette Bldg.	Chicago, Ill.
Douglass, Kingman		Holland, Mich.
Downing, Samuel K.	817 Kenilworth Ave.	Oak Park, Ill.
Duncan, Asa N.	—	Higginsville, Mo.
Farnsworth, Austin M.		Sheffield, Ala.
Fay, Samuel P.	2707 Routh St.	Dallas, Tex.
Fell, Nelson	2 Otis Place	Boston, Mass.
Fleck, Abe H.		Warrenton, Va.
Fontaine, Hugh L.	1839 Overton Park Ave.	Cincinnati, Ohio.
Foster, Frederick V.	—	Memphis, Tenn.
Frierson, Samuel G.		East Orange, N. J.
Graham, Russell	835 N. Comstock Ave.	Madison, Wis.
Gray, Denver F.	1414 Eighth St.	Whittier, Cal.
Guilbert, Horace M.	21 Sylvan Ave.	New Orleans, La.
Hammond, Leonard C.	252 Broadway	West Newton, Mass.
Hammond, D. Q.		San Francisco, Cal.
Hamilton, James L.	5207 Walnut St.	
Hardy, Donald E.	—	Philadelphia, Pa.
Henderson, John C.		Amherst, Mass.
Hill, Maury	5505 Lindell Blvd.	Americus, Ga.
Hirth, Frederick K.	Killed in action	St. Louis, Mo.
Hoel, Orton F.	—	
Hooper, Klein L.		Eveleth, Minn.
Hotton, Harold J.		Roanoke, Ala.
Houghton, Earle		Portville, N. Y.
		Claremont, Cal.

149

Name	Address / Status	Location
Howard, Thomas D.	329 West Ave. 51	Los Angeles, Cal.
Hudson, Charles F.	205 North 6th St.	Henryetta, Okla.
Hughey, Paul H.	Killed in action	—
Hume, Alan P.	1781 Columbia Road	Washington, D. C.
Husted, Merle R.	— —	Roodhouse, Ill.
Jannopoulo, R. Stockton	15 East 35th St.	New York City.
Jervey, Thomas M.	7 Pitts St.	Charleston, S. C.
Jones, Kirtly	—	Boyds, Md.
Kelty, Asher E.	Killed in action	—
Kenneson, Edward R.	Died Jan. 10, 1919	—
Kenney, George C.	4 Egremont Read	Brookline, Mass.
Kincaid, Alvin C.	General Delivery	Orleans, Ind.
Kirby, French	1847 Parkwood Pl.N.W.	Washington, D. C.
Lambert, John H.	Harvard Club	Boston, Mass.
Lawson, Alfred W.	1060 72nd St.	Brooklyn, N. Y.
Lawson, Walter R.	— —	Birmingham, Ala.
Lowry, Francis B.	Killed in action	—
Mangan, Harry N.	57 Chestnut St.	Salem, N. J.
Martin, J. Roberts	Bank of Italy	San Francisco, Cal.
Mayer, George W.	808 Church St.	Phoenixville, Pa.
Mayes, Howard G.	— —	Charleston, W. Va.
Merrill, George B.	105 E. Main St.	North East Pa.
Moran, George S.	134 Lincoln Place	Brooklyn, N. Y.
Moran, William J.	1677 Harrison St.	Frankford, Philadelphia, Pa.
Orr, John C.	— —	Babylon, L. I., N. Y.
Perry, Harley	— —	Rockdale, Tex.
Pope, John B., Jr.	c/o R. S. Beard	Littlefield, Tex.
Powell, Leon W.	Lamonde Ave.	Durham, N. C.
Reynolds, Clearton H.	264 West 57th St.	New York City
Reynolds, John N.	c/o Adj.Gen.,U.S.Army	Washington, D. C.
Richardson, John S., Jr.	24 Alaska St.	Boston, Mass.
Ripley, Roy S.	201 Toledo St.	San Antonio, Tex.
Roper, Kenyon	Killed in Action	—
Russell, Linus E.	—	Welshfield, Ohio.
Ruth, Lloyd A.	1501 11th Ave. South	Minneapolis, Minn.
Scanlon, Martin F.	c/o Adj.Gen.,U.S.Army	Washington, D. C.
Schaffner, Herbert A.	Killed in action	Hummelstown, Pa.
Schilling, Franz F.	Lion Dry Goods Co.	—
Schricker, John W.	Killed in action	Toledo, Ohio.
Scott, Robert G.	Killed in action	—
Sebring, Raymond R.	1282 Maple Ave.	—
Seymour, Alonzo M.	314 Oak St.	Peekskill, N. Y.
Sieper, Frederick E.	319 North 6th St.	Passaic, N. J.
Snyder, John H.	2501 Mallon Ave.	Reading, Pa.
Stone, Ralph W.	—	Spokane, Wash.
Strahm, Victor H.	361 Ocean Ave.	Bowling Green, Ky.
Sutherland, Clarke S.	PressIll.Co.,142W.23dSt.	Brooklyn, N. Y.
Suydam, James	6211 Christian St.	New York City.
Sweeney, Raymond W.	2718 Laclede Ave.	Philadelphia, Pa.
Tabachnik, Abraham	—	St. Louis, Mo.
Terry, Prentice M.	512 S. Harvard Blvd.	Louisville, Ky.
Thorne, Harold W.	50 South Cedar St.	Los Angeles, Cal.
Van Heuvel, John W.	—	Mobile, Ala.
Verwohlt, Howard W.	11 Bigelow St.	Tiltonville, Ohio.
Wallis, James E.	124 Wesley Ave.	Cambridge, Mass.
Warren, Horatio A.	—	Buffalo, N. Y.
Wasson, Roy J.	Killed in accident	Camden, N. Y.
Watson, Harold S.		—

Weisbach, Arthur H.	24 Bradley Road	Tacoma, Wash.
Westover, Bernard O.	—	Rushville, Neb.
White, William A.	Killed in action	—
Whitaker, John H.	140 College Ave.	Davenport, Iowa.
Wienges, Paul C.	814 Telfair St.	Augusta, Ga.
Wilbur, F. Vaughn,	1312 Maryland Ave.	Los Angeles, Cal.
Williamson, Joseph F.	— —	Sebastopol, Cal.
Wise, John E.		Durand, Wis.
Withstandley, Victor	270 Clinton Ave.	Brooklyn N. Y.
Young, Clyde	621 West Paradise	Vernon, Tex.

o o o

LIST OF MEN.

Airey, Harold L.	Pvt. 1st Cl.	New Haven, Conn.
* Anderson, Ralph R.	M. E.	Little Rock, Ark.
Angle, John S.	Pvt.	Pittsburg, Pa.
Bernardini, Stanislas	Pvt.	Auburn, N. Y.
* Blain, Samuel R.	Sgt.	Sweet Springs, Mo.
Blair, Charles E.	Pvt.	Kingsville, Md.
Bletsch, Charles E.	Pvt.	Highland Park, Ill.
* Boardman, John A.	Pvt.	Toledo, Ohio.
Boyd, Fred C.	Pvt	Christiana, Pa.
* Bretz, John C.	Cpl.	Morrison, Ill.
* Brittain, Robert A.	Chfr.	St. Joseph, Mo.
* Broderick, Martin A.	Pvt.	Frankford, Philadelphia, Pa
* Brown, Murdock,	Cpl.	Corpus Christi, Texas.
Brown, Willis S.	Pvt. 1st Cl.	Cleveland, Ohio.
* Bryan, George D.	Chfr.	West Point, Miss.
* Butler, Cletus N.	Pvt 1st Cl.	Attawa, Ill.
Carpenter, Julien O.	Pvt	Newman, Ga.
* Carrigan, Scott E.	Sgt. 1st Cl.	Fort Dodge, Iowa.
(Avi. Mech.)		
* Church, Charles J.	Pvt. 1st Cl.	Minneapolis, Minn.
* Clark, Howard L.	Pvt. 1st Cl.	Windsor, Mo.
Coombs, Leslie B.	Pvt.	Chicago, Ill.
* Creviston, Clyde C.	Pvt.	Matoon, Ill.
Cottier, William F.	Pvt. 1st Cl.	Passaic, N. J.
Daly, Edward A.	Cpl.	Brooklyn, N. Y.
* Dantrey, Attely E.	Pvt. 1st Cl.	Cecil, Pa.
Davidson, Samuel	Pvt.	New York City.
* Dempsey, Charles O.	Pvt.	Wilmington, Del.
* Dimmit, Rex U.	Pvt. 1st Cl.	Ottumwa, Iowa.
Dolan, Thomas J.	Pvt.	Providence, R. I.
Dowd, Patrick J	Pvt.	Holyoke, Mass.
Ebeltoft, Carl T.	Pvt,	Lake Park, Minn.
Eberhart, Albert L.	Pvt. 1st Cl.	Norden, Nebr.
* Ellis, James H.	Cpl.	Chester, Mass.
Erickson, August L.	Pvt.	Parkers Prairie, Minn.
Farley, Arthur C.	Pvt.	Newark, N. J.
Fedder, Gus J.	Pvt.	West Haven, Conn.
Fisher, Milo M.	Pvt.	Owatonna, Minn.
Fox, Paul O.	Pvt.	Bucyrus, Ohio.
Fraser, Thomas E.	Pvt.	Fall River, Mass.
* Frey, Robert M.	Chfr. 1st Cl.	Chambersburg, Pa.

* Friang, Henry G.	Cpl.	Madison, Wis.
Gilchrist, Philip A.	Pvt.	Providence, R. I.
Gilmore, Alfred	Pvt.	Philadelphia, Pa.
Hager, Benjamin F.	Pvt.	El Dorado, Okla.
Hanger, Curtis E.	Pvt.	West Lafayette, Ind.
Hansen, Edwin M.	Pvt.	Racine, Wis.
* Hanton, John	Pvt. 1st Cl.	Hamilton, Ontario, Canada
* Hays, Carl L.	Cook	Galena, Mo.
Head, William C.	Pvt. 1st Cl.	Stockton, Cal.
Hoban, Edward J	Pvt.	Chicago, Ill.
Hott, Earl S.	Cpl.	Asheville, Ohio.
Huggins, Waldo J.	Pvt.	Honey Grove, Texas.
* Irvin, James B.	Cpl.	San Antonio, Texas.
Jennings, Ralph E.	Sgt. 1st Cl.	Cawker City, Kans.
* Jones, Charles J.	Pvt.	Flushing, L. I. N. Y.
Judge, William R.	Pvt.	Fall River, Mass.
Kjelleberg, Knute	Pvt.	Hazel Run, Minn.
Kline, Edwin S.	Pvt.	Tulsa, Okla.
Kloska, Frank T.	Pvt.	South Bend, Ind.
Koehler, Frank J.	Pvt.	Paola, Kans
* Lawrence, Abbott A.	Pvt. 1st Cl.	Manchester, N. H.
* Lee, Calvin J.	Cpl.	Georgiana, Ala.
* Lewis, Frank M.	Cpl.	Warren, Ohio.
* MacBrannan, Elgie	Chfr.	Bryan, Ohio.
* MacDonald, Donald E.	Chfr.	Deer Lodge, Mont.
* Maggio, Pedro	Pvt.	North Judson, Ind.
* Manger, Michael	Sgt. 1st Cl.	Detroit, Mich.
Martin, John F.	Pvt.	Flat Creek, Tenn.
* Matthews, James G.	Sgt. 1st Cl.	Greenville, Texas.
* McAbee, Nestor J.	Sgt. 1st Cl.	San Francisco, Calif.
(Avi. Mech.)		
* McAnally, Ray	M. E.	Glendive, Mont.
(Avi. Mech.)		
* McCarthy, Aloysius A.	Sgt. 1st Cl.	Dennison, Texas.
* McCray, Buckley L.	Sgt. 1st Cl.	Oilman, Iowa.
* McDonald, Columbus P.	Pvt.	Vernon, Texas.
McEldowney, Frank E.	Chfr.	Upper Sandusky, Ohio.
* McGuyre, Vernon T.	Pvt.	Richland, Texas.
McNutt, William	Pvt.	Chicago, Ill.
* McQuillin, Elmer E.	Pvt. 1st Cl.	Buffalo, N. Y.
Megill, Linn S.	Pvt.	Denver, Col.
* Merrill, William C.	Sgt. 1st Cl.	Chicago, Ill.
* Mershon, Milton M.	Pvt. 1st Cl.	Walters, Okla.
* Millar, Lloyd J.	Pvt.	Buffalo, N. Y.
* Mobley, Leroy	Sgt.	Richmond, Ind.
* Moon, Charles T.	Sgt.	El Paso, Texas.
* Morris, Peter T.	Pvt.	South Brownsville, Pa.
* Morrow, John G.	Sgt.	Le Compte, La.
* Moxley, Edward B.	Chfr.	Greensburg, Pa.
Muir, George A.	Sgt.	Memphis, Tenn.
Munson, Frank L.	Cook	Walridge, Ohio.
* Murphy, Seymour C.	Cpl.	South Sioux City, Nebr.
* Myers, Willie O.	Pvt.	Dallas, Texas.
* Newman, Ernest	Sgt.	Lake Providence, La.
* Niehuis, Jacob H.	Sgt.	La Porte, Ind.
* Norden, Arthur G.	Cpl.	Defiance, Ohio.
O'Brien, Maurice D.	Chfr.	East Liverpool, Ohio.
* O'Connell, Michael J.	Sgt.	New London, Wis.

* O'Neill, Daniel E.	Cpl.	Niagara Falls, N. Y.
* Osborne, Earl M.	Pvt. 1st Cl.	Meade, Kans.
* Parady, Grant	Sgt. 1st Cl.	Council Bluffs, Iowa.
Paulus, William H. A.	Sgt.	Atlantic City, N. J.
* Penney, Claude L.	Sgt.	Waupaca, Wis.
Pettitt, Eldon C.	Pvt.	Marion, Ind.
* Pierson, Edwin K.	Pvt. 1st Cl.	Benedict, Nebr.
* Pierson, Nels S.	Sgt.	Benedict, Nebr.
Plumb, John H.	Pvt.	Sylvan Grove, Kans.
* Poole, Peter J.	Chfr.	Aurora, Ill.
* Powers, Maurice	Cook	Cleveland, Ohio.
* Purdy, Charles R.	Sgt. 1st Cl.	Two Harbors, Minn.
* Qualls, Lewellen B.	Pvt.	Terre Haute, Ind.
* Ragusa, Anthony	Cook	Houston, Texas.
* Rainboth, Guy E.	Chfr. 1st Cl.	Ogdensburg, N. Y.
* Ratcliffe, Ronald G.	Sgt. 1st Cl.	Vincennes, Ind.
* Ray, Thane R.	Sgt. 1st Cl.	Handley, Texas.
Rhinefield, Lewis C.	Pvt.	Beland, Fla.
* Richards, Frank	Pvt.	Mount Vernon, Pa.
* Richardson, Nicholas K.	Pvt. 1st Cl.	Turtle Creek, Pa.
* Richardson, Oscar N.	Sgt. 1st Cl.	Rome, Ga.
* Rike, Willard G.	Sgt.	Farmersville, Texas.
* Riske, Thomas A.	Sgt.	St. Louis, Mo.
* Rooks, William M.	Pvt.	Enfield, Ill.
* Rowe, Harry E.	Sgt. 1st Cl.	Aurora, Ill.
* Rucker, Melvin E.	Pvt.	Chatfield, Minn.
* Russell, Max	Pvt. 1st Cl.	Chicago, Ill.
* Sahm, Albert J.	Sgt. 1st Cl.	Linton, Ind.
* Sanders, Frank H.	Sgt. 1st Cl.	Marshall, Texas.
* Schannep, Aden D.	Chfr.	South Whitley, Ind.
* Schuelke, Albert R.	M. E.	Dennison, Texas.
* Schwalm, Morris F.	Chfr. 1st Cl.	Alma, Kans.
* Silva, Alwin W.	Pvt.	Oakland, Calif.
* Sinclair, William W.	Sgt.	Waycross, Ga.
* Smith, Labanna J.	Sgt. 1st Cl.	Oil City, Pa.
* Smyth, William L.	Sgt.	Connelsville, Pa.
* Snow, Malt N.	Sgt. 1st Cl.	Brownwood, Ala.
(Avi. Mech.)		
* Soper, Eldred L.	Cpl.	Bay City, Mich.
* Sorensen, David C.	Cpl.	Boelus, Nebr.
* Souder, Harold	M. E.	Detroit, Mich.
Southern, Wesley	Pvt.	Bellingham, Wash.
Spence, William H.	Pvt.	Franklin, Mass.
* Spindle, Buell Y.	Chfr.	White Wright, Texas.
* Sproule, Stewart G.	Pvt.	Custer, Mich.
* Stanley, Raymond E.	Cpl.	Garden Grove, Iowa.
* Stecker, Ernest Jr.	Sgt.	San Carlos, Ariz.
* Steffel, Frank A.	Pvt. 1st Cl.	Milwaukee, Wis.
Strauss, Charles W.	Pvt.	Mahaffey, Pa.
* Straw, Noel B.	Pvt.	Cement City, Mich.
* Sweeney, James W.	Cpl	Boerne, Texas.
* Sylvester, Joseph A.	Cook	Macon, Ga.
* Taylor, William	Pvt. 1st Cl.	Kansas City, Mo.
* Thompson, Walter L.	Sgt.	Piper City, Ill.
* Toney, William S.	Pvt. 1st Cl.	Colorado Springs, Co
* Trone, Millard V.	Chfr.	San Jose, Calif.
* Turnley, Richard P.	Pvt. 1st Cl.	Shrevesport, La.
* Umbenhour, John S.	Cpl.	Fort Worth, Texas.

* Unton, Harry A.	Chfr. 1st Cl.	Fayette, Iowa.
* Waits, Troy E.	Pvt. 1st Cl.	Dennison, Texas.
* Waldo, John F.	Pvt. 1st Cl.	New Orleans, La.
* Walker, Aaron L.	Pvt.	Marion, Ill.
* Walker, Buck	Chfr.	Bogota, Texas.
* Walker, Frances I.	M. E.	Mesquite, Texas.
* Walker, Orlan E.	Pvt.	Marion, Ill.
* Walter, Harry L.	Chfr.	Rising City, Nebr.
* Walldren, Arthur H.	Chfr. 1st Cl.	Congress Park, Ill.
* Ward, Bert C.	Chfr. 1st Cl.	Gary, Ind.
* Warner, Marvin J.	Chfr. 1st Cl.	Bryan, Ohio.
* Way, James L.	Sgt.	Wahoo, Nebr.
* White, Willie L.	Cook	San Saba, Texas.
* Wicker, Debert W.	Pvt.	Blue Ridge, Texas.
* Wickins, Charles K.	Sgt. 1st Cl.	St. Louis, Mo.
* Wieczorek, Clesmer	Pvt. 1st Cl.	Detroit, Mich.
* Wilkinson, Don E.	Cpl.	Williamson, W. Va.
* Williams, Thomas	Cpl.	Billings, Mont.
* Wills, Jess M.	Chfr. 1st Cl.	Winchester, Ill.
* Winters, Calvin C.	Pvt.	Stephensville, Texas.
* Womack, Nelson T.	Sgt. 1st Cl.	Marshall, Texas.
Woods, Joseph A.	Pvt.	Lyons, Ky.
* Wortham, Harry M.	Chfr.	Cherokee, Okla.
* Wullenwaber, Charles L.	Pvt.	Harper, Kans.
* Yeager, Roscoe	Pvt.	Manckport, Ind.

MEDICAL DETACHMENT.

* Shivers, George M.	Sgt.	Wheeling, W. Va.
* Shoulders, Bratton F.	Pvt. 1st Cl.	Frisco, Texas.
* Sorrels, Ed. S.	Pvt. 1st Cl.	Fort Worth, Texas.
* Vosburgh, Rollie	Pvt. 1st Cl.	Toledo, Ohio.

ORDNANCE DETACHMENT.

Pyle, George H.	Pvt.	New York City, N. Y.
Fyhrie, George E.	Cpl.	St. Paul, Min.
Garvey, Bernard S.	Cpl.	Chicago, Ills.
Hayes, Edwin J.	Pvt.	Worcester, Mass.

INTELLIGENCE DETACHMENT.

Easterbrook, Wilfred G.	Sgt.	Seattle, Wash.
Mohler, Herbert S.	Cpl.	Canonsburg, Pa.

LOSSES SINCE LEAVING UNITED STATES.

Augustus, Willard R.	Pvt.	Scranton, Iowa.	Died 1/16/19
Chatelle, Charles F.	Pvt.	Wichita, Kans.	Died 1/16/19
* Chrisman, Roy E.	Pvt.	Normal, Ill.	Trnsf. 10/6/18
Conklin, Glenn A.	Pvt.	Denver, Col.	Trnsf. 1/27/19
Culliton, William P.	Pvt.	Troy, N. Y.	Trnsf. 1/27/19
* Dean, Fred E.	Pvt.	Tioga, Wis.	Trnsf. 2/26/19
* Demaray, Harry N.	Chfr.	Pipestone, Minn.	Trnsf. 10/2/18
* Peyrer, Frank J.	Pvt.	Westhoff, Texas.	Trnsf. 8/6/18
Fisher, John L.	Pvt.	Dayton, Ohio.	Trnsf. 11/14/18

Name	Rank	Location	Status	Date
* French, Floyd W.	Pvt.	Dayton, Ohio.	Trnsf.	10/6/18
Godfrey, Carlton	Pvt.	Atlantic City, N. J.	Trnsf.	10/9/18
* Harrison, Paul D.	Pvt.	Main Rock, Ala.	Trnsf.	4/4/18
Hulet, David W.	Pvt.	Driggs, Idaho.	Trnsf.	1/27/19
* Knepp, Luther O.	Pvt.	Bernham, Pa.	Trnsf.	10/6/18
* Lewis, Lelfy S.	Sgt. 1st Cl.	Faxon, Okla.	Trnsf.	1/27/19
* Meredith, Claire	Pvt. 1st Cl.	McKeesport, Pa.	Trnsf.	7/19/18
Metcalfe, Thomas V.	Pvt.	Lotus, Calif.	Trnsf.	1/27/19
* Miessner, Frank	Pvt.	Huntingburg, Ind.	Trnsf.	4/4/18
* Monson, Ralph E.	Sgt. 1st Cl.	York, Nebr.	Trnsf.	8/19/18
* Moon, Charles S.	Pvt.	South Bend, Ind.	Died	6/10/18
Moore, Marion E.	Pvt. 1st Cl.	Morgantown, W. Va.	Died	2/19/19
* Moreland, William B.	Cpl.	Decatur, Texas.	Trnsf.	6/1/18
* Newton, Horace O.	Pvt.	Loraine, Texas.	Trnsf.	2/13/18
* O'Connor, William K.	Pvt.	Sparrow Point, Md.	Trnsf.	3/7/18
* Olson, John L.	Cpl.	St. Joseph, Mo.	Trnsf.	8/15/18
* Peterson, Glen	Sgt.	Bryan, Ohio.	Comm	2/20/18
* Rebillot, Lawrence J.	Pvt.	Louisville, Ohio.	Trnsf.	4/4/18
Richardson, Carl J.	Pvt.	Springfield, Ohio.	Trnsf.	10/6/18
* Sherrill, Paul W.	Sgt.	Temple, Texas.	Trnsf.	8/15/18
* Smith, Ray F.	Pvt.	Fond du Lac, Wis.	Trnsf.	12/18/18
* Soderlund, Gustave	Sgt.	Escanaba, Mich.	Trnsf.	4/4/18
* Stringer, Charles M.	Pvt.	Lincoln, Ill.	Trnsf.	5/21/18
Threlkeld, Howard M.	Pvt.	Phoenix, Ariz.	Trnsf.	10/9/18
Van Kirk, Bryant F.	M. E.	Vincennes, Ind.	Died	1/19/19
Vermillion, Russell T.	Chfr.	Higginsville, Mo.	Trnsf.	8/15/18
Walling, Thomas D.	Pvt.	South Bend, Ind.	Trnsf.	10/9/18
Ward, Roy	Pvt.	Bradstown, Ky.	Trnsf.	10/6/18

*) Came over in squadron.

PHOTOGRAPHIC SECTION No. 2.

COMMANDING OFFICERS.

Barnhill, William A. 2nd Lt. AS., USA. From Sept. 19, 1918.
Suydam, James S. 1st Lt. AS., USA, From June 15, 1918 to Sept. 18, 1918.

PRESENT ENLISTED PERSONNEL.

Angelo, Alan	Cpl.	Atlantic City, N. J.
Atchison, Ernest S.	Pvt. 1st Cl.	Washington, D. C.
Baker, George J.	Pvt. 1st Cl.	Linton, Ind.
Blades, Le Roy	Sgt.	Chicago, Ill.
Brennan, Robert J.	Pvt. 1st Cl.	Medina, N. Y.
Bronson, Ira L.	Pvt. 1st Cl.	Seattle, Wash.
Buttasi, Galdino	Cpl.	West Hoboken, N. J.
Chadderton, William	Sgt. 1st Cl.	Sharon, Pa.
Cheesman, Arthur E.	Cpl.	Brooklyn, N. Y.
Conlon, Ernest L.	Pvt. 1st Cl.	Ithaca, N. Y.
Dahl, Henry H.	Pvt. 1st Cl.	Chicago, Ill.
Demmon, Ralph W.	Cpl.	Grand Rapids, Mich.
Drehs, William F.	Cpl.	Sassamansville, Pa.
Harding, Lloyd E.	Cpl.	Berwyn, Ill.
Harper, Ira C.	Chfr.	Washington, D. C.
Johnston, Merton F.	Pvt. 1st Cl.	Corinth, N. Y.
Lacy, Elmer D.	Pvt. 1st Cl.	Cowles, Neb.

155

Lantz, Charles E.	Cpl.	Westminster, Md.
Merrill, Harold V.	Cpl.	Maywood, Ill.
Miner, Gilbert P.	Chfr. 1st Cl.	Madison, Wis.
Remley, John H.	Cpl.	Berwick, Pa.
Ridder, John E.	Pvt. 1st Cl.	Germania, Grant, W.Va
Rogers, Philip W.	Cpl.	Thurmont, Md.
Scott, Graham H.	Pvt. 1st Cl.	Rochester, N. Y.
Strauch, Donald W.	Pvt. 1st Cl.	Champaign, Ill.
Stone, James	Pvt. 1st Cl.	Rochester, N. Y.
Stringer, Charles M.	Sgt.	Peoria, Ill.

TRANSFERRED FROM SECTION.

Abernethy, Harry C.	Sgt.
Campbell, Alvan G.	Pvt.
Clemens, Walter C.	Sgt.
Eversole, William K.	Cpl.
Flitcraft, Elwood L.	Chfr.
Morrison, Frank E.	Pvt.
Peel, Clifford E.	Cpl.
Sears, Joseph M.	Pvt. 1st Cl.
Vandenhoecke, Lucien E.	Pvt. 1st Cl.